Freire,
Teaching,
and Learning

Studies in the
Postmodern Theory of Education

Joe L. Kincheloe and Shirley R. Steinberg
General Editors

Vol. 350

PETER LANG
New York • Washington, D.C./Baltimore • Bern
Frankfurt am Main • Berlin • Brussels • Vienna • Oxford

Mariana Souto-Manning

Freire,
Teaching,
and Learning

CULTURE CIRCLES ACROSS CONTEXTS

PETER LANG
New York • Washington, D.C./Baltimore • Bern
Frankfurt am Main • Berlin • Brussels • Vienna • Oxford

Library of Congress Cataloging-in-Publication Data

Souto-Manning, Mariana.
Freire, teaching, and learning: culture circles across contexts /
Mariana Souto-Manning.
p. cm. — (Counterpoints: studies in the postmodern theory of education; v. 350)
Includes bibliographical references and index.
1. Critical pedagogy. 2. Multicultural education—United States.
3. Multicultural education—Brazil. 4. Freire, Paulo, 1921–1997. I. Title.
LC196.5.U6S68   370.11'5—dc22   2009036983
ISBN 978-1-4331-0406-0
ISSN 1058-1634

Bibliographic information published by **Die Deutsche Nationalbibliothek.**
Die Deutsche Nationalbibliothek lists this publication in the "Deutsche
Nationalbibliografie"; detailed bibliographic data is available
on the Internet at http://dnb.d-nb.de/.

The paper in this book meets the guidelines for permanence and durability
of the Committee on Production Guidelines for Book Longevity
of the Council of Library Resources.

© 2010 Peter Lang Publishing, Inc., New York
29 Broadway, 18th floor, New York, NY 10006
www.peterlang.com

Printed in the United States of America

I dedicate this book to the lives and legacies of two powerful critical pedagogues—

Paulo Freire

(1921 - 1997)

&

Joe L. Kincheloe

(1950 - 2008)

—and to all educators who were inspired by their work. May we continue honoring their work in our classrooms and beyond.

Contents

Acknowledgments

I would like to acknowledge **ALL** of those with whom I have had the pleasure of teaching and learning. In particular...

Instituto Capibaribe

Since I was a little girl, I have asked questions. As I look back, I realize that my problem-posing approach to learning and living was shaped by my schooling at Instituto Capibaribe. I would like to acknowledge the teachers and administrators of this progressive, liberatory school in Recife, Brazil. In particular, the influence of its co-founders, Paulo Freire and Raquel de Crasto (my principal from kindergarten to eighth grade), on my education and the way I came to read words and worlds.

My Mentors

As I emigrated from Brazil to the United States, I encountered two supporting, caring and committed educators, who believed in me and in the work I do. There are no words that can express my enormous gratitude and admiration for my mentors and friends—Betsy Rymes (University of Pennsylvania) and Celia Genishi (Teachers College, Columbia University)—who continuously inspire and challenge me.

The Participants and Co-Authors of this Book

This book could not have been written without the consent, involvement, and kindness of its participants. You have been important parts of my life as a critical educator. While some people may have thought of Freirean culture circles as a thing of the past, you lived the critical cycle with me, and your powerful stories and experiences of change and transformation are what make this book so powerful. I offer you my sincere gratitude!

First, I must acknowledge the voices, courage and inspiration provided by the children in my first- and second-grade classrooms. They dared to ask questions, to confront situations, and to expand the borders of what was allowed in order to promote what was just. Never doubt that you have the power to change the world. You do!

Second, I recognize the kindness of the participants in the adult literacy program sponsored by the government of my native Pernambuco, Brazil. Thank you for teaching me lessons on humility, hope, and love. As you strove to change your worlds, you changed mine.

Third, as I moved to educating teachers in U.S. universities (University of South Carolina—Columbia, University of Georgia, and Teachers College, Columbia University), I embraced learning all over again, collectively. I acknowledge my early childhood teacher education students. I hope that the lessons we learned together are making your classrooms more just spaces.

Finally, as I engaged in in-service teacher education, I was kindly joined by two groups of teachers who made themselves vulnerable and embraced the power of collective, critical, and transformative learning. For over two years, the teachers at the Child Development Lab at the McPhaul Center joined me in Freirean culture circles. We laughed, we cried, we learned together. I acknowledge the voices and contributions of all, but particularly those of Amy Evans, Siobian Minish, Christy Mitchell, Christy Cook, Marie Covington, Courtney King, Phillip Baumgarner, Tricia Amberg, and Anjanette Russell. In addition, together with colleagues, co-authors, and friends, Betsy Rymes (University of Pennsylvania) and Melisa Cahnmann-Taylor (University of Georgia), over six years, I learned alongside bilingual teachers who acted up and performed change in their own contexts. I acknowledge all participants and in particular "Sonia," who is now a kindergarten teacher in a public school in the Southeast, and my co-authors in sections of Chapter 7 of this book—Melisa Cahnmann-Taylor, Jaime L. Dice, and Jennifer Wooten.

Supportive Individuals

As I wrote this book, I was inspired by the words of educators whose work promotes collaborative, dialogic, and transformative education. JoBeth Allen, William Ayers, Sonia Nieto, and Ira Shor not only inspired this book, but read the text with care and offered words of support as well as questions to be considered. I sincerely thank Ira Shor for his insightful Foreword and William Ayers for his inspirational Afterword. I would also like to thank JoBeth Allen and Sonia Nieto for their supportive words and actions.

I acknowledge the role of Shirley Steinberg, who attended one of my presentations at an American Educational Research Association conference and identified the importance of publishing this book. In addition, I thank graduate students at the University of Georgia—Meghan Dove, Boh Young Lee, Melissa Scott Kozak—and at Teachers College, Columbia University—Mei Ying Tan—who helped me with multiple tasks which brought this project to reality. Finally, I offer my gratitude to Sophie Appel for her professional support, careful editing, encouragement, and patience throughout the process.

Funding Agencies

This work would not have been possible without the generous support of the following funders: Tinker Foundation; the U.S. Department of Education, Transition to Teaching Program, and Office of Special Education Program; the University of Georgia Research Foundation; and the National Council of Teachers of English (NCTE) Research Foundation, Cultivating New Voices (CNV) Program.

Support Communities

I acknowledge my CNV family—Anne Haas Dyson, Arnetha Ball, Benji Chang, Carmen Mercado, Carol Lee, Celia Genishi, Colleen

Fairbanks, David Kirkland, Detra Price-Dennis, Django Paris, Jason Irizarry, JoBeth Allen, Juan Guerra, Kafi Kumasi, Marcelle Haddix, Maria Franquiz, Maria Torres-Guzman, Mary Rojas, Rachelle Dail, Sonia Nieto, Tambra Jackson, Valerie Kinloch, Veronica Valdez, and Violet Harris. Thank you for being there for me and for inspiring me!

While I will not attempt to list names, I want to acknowledge my friends and colleagues at the Early Childhood Education Assembly (NCTE), at the University of South Carolina - Columbia, at the University of Georgia, and at Teachers College, Columbia University.

My Family

Most importantly, I must acknowledge the paramount role of my family. *A Suely Valois, José Carlos Souto (in memorian), Maria do Carmo Souto, Thiago, Bernardo, Juliana, Jacineide, & Amara, muito obrigada por tudo. Vocês foram e continuam sendo extremamente importantes para mim!*

Dwight, Lucas, and Thomas—thank you for your love, support, and belief that everything is possible, that change is needed, that differences and diversities need to be appreciated for their beauties and strengths, and that education is truly transformative. We must always ask hard questions and engage in dialogue. I am committed to make this world a better place and am thrilled that you join and inspire me every day!

Foreword

by Ira Shor

The Graduate Center, City University of New York

When Paulo Freire died suddenly in a Brazil hospital on May 2, 1997, many colleagues and admirers skipped a breath as the sad news spread around the world. His remarkable "pedagogy of the oppressed" had captured the imagination of countless educators across many borders and languages, in elite universities as well as in peasant villages and factory towns. (This literacy method also captured the ire of the Brazilian elite and military whose April 1964 coup jailed Freire, demolished his program, and exiled him for 15 years from the land and people he loved.) In constant demand until his final day, Freire traveled and traveled, during and after his exile—humorously describing himself as "a vagabond of the obvious" and "a peregrine of revolution"—to encourage young teachers especially that another world is possible, one less cruel, less violent, and more equal. This short man's charismatic manner enveloped the gatherings he attended partly for the hope he embodied and partly because he practiced what he called "humble militance" or "militant humility." Unassuming and unaffected, Freire preferred not to lecture but rather invited the audience to put issues on the table for dialogue. He hoped that his visits would promote consolidation, for diverse and divided local activists to coalesce into an alliance for opposition.

The passing of a charismatic figure like Paulo Freire, whose life and work generated a school of thought and practice, leaves a hole that no other social justice educator can fill. His foundational work in critical pedagogy continues to inform many efforts in teaching. But, the foundation he articulated in writing—in talks, in programs, and by personal example—leaves many questions of theory and application unanswered. This unfinished map requires another generation to invent its way forward in this undertaking. In the years since Freire died, this mapping-out has been happening, fortunately. In many places, smart and creative educators are patiently rewriting "the pedagogy of the oppressed." Freire urged such reinvention for all those inspired by his example, insisting that the only way to copy him was not to copy him but rather to resituate the practice in the times and places we inhabit.

This continuing reinvention of Freire is at the heart of Mariana Souto-Manning's book *Freire, Teaching, and Learning: Culture Circles Across Contexts*. In these chapters, Souto-Manning examines Freirean problem-posing at distinct sites: a diverse primary school classroom for six-and-seven-year-olds, culture circles for adults in Brazil, and pre-service/in-service teacher education in the U.S. She not only pictures culture circles at work in different settings, but also outlines some similar starting points which define the practice: basing the curriculum in the students' language use, conditions, interests, and themes; putting dialogic inquiry at the center of the learning process instead of teacherly monologue; adapting the lessons to follow and draw out the cognitive activity of the students. She wisely keeps in front of us the complexity of the practice: "Through the exploration of relevant issues and themes, culture circle participants engage in inquiry, questioning, and charting a course of action. As they problema-

tize themes and issues, old knowledge and assumptions collide with
new knowledge. Participants can then construct their own knowledge
in a critical manner...[S]tudents' experiences are invited, valued, and
central to the construction of meaning. This is not a simple process,
however"(pp. 23–25).

Souto-Manning reports the nuances and difficulties of making the
dialogic process work. For example, her first-grade class is a mixed-
ability group which she chooses to teach without remedial or ESL
"pull-outs" that stigmatize some children. This section is an especially
valuable report in this age of runaway tracking and standardized testing. In the elementary school where she taught the whole class as a
culture circle, there was a panorama of stakeholders with whom ne-
gotiations were required for the process to take off: "The major difficulties I experienced were (1) proving to parents this [culture circle
approach] would benefit all children and not just serve as a gift to
those receiving remedial classes/services, and (2) coordinating my
classroom time with the other teachers...Upon gathering the support
from 17 of the 19 parents, I went on to talk with the principal...She
seemed reluctant at first, but upon hearing of the parent support I had
gathered, she agreed to consider...The main obstacle was to convince
the teacher [of gifted students] that all children could learn in an inquiry-based curriculum" (pp. 85–86). She had to convince skeptical
parents, teachers, and a principal that a new model would work. Such
passages illuminate the local politics of transformative teaching
where social justice educators negotiate change in dense institutional
settings. Another telling moment of negotiated conflict in these narratives is when the adult "literants" in a Brazilian culture circle used the
process to address issues of most concern to them, in this case gender,
in a locale where patriarchy restricted women's education because
"girls have to stay home and help their mothers." Souto-Manning reports how the culture circle mobilized such a "generative theme" so
that the patriarchal limits could be challenged in the literacy dialogue.
In the third site of culture circles she reports, pre-service/in-service
teacher education in a university, the consequences are equally re-
vealing. Schoolteachers in America have little or no opportunity to

come of age familiar with critical-democratic practices because the classrooms they emerge from as students are predominantly teacher-centered and test-driven. Providing teacher education which experientially models the culture circle approach is of signal value in reforming teacher preparation. It helps distribute concrete experiences of alternative practices which make critical pedagogy legible and feasible.

From these varied experiences of culture circles, Souto-Manning draws some important lessons for teachers who agree that student experience should be the primary subject matter: "...while it would be easiest to have students volunteer the most oppressive aspects of their lives in these settings, they are initially reluctant to do so. To create a community of learners based on trust and respect, I suggest that it is helpful for teachers to position themselves as ethnographers, studying the cultural practices within and across the communities learners inhabit. By documenting the most urgent struggles experienced by many of the participants of a culture circle and codifying those experiences in a generative theme...facilitators open up opportunities for students to name, problematize and deconstruct issues which are paramount in their lives"(pp. 37–38). Souto-Manning follows here Freire's notion that the teacher should begin as a student of the students, equipping herself to lead a critical culture circle by first learning from the students the material conditions of their lives. From this ethnographic study, the teacher discovers generative themes which become the subject matters for problem-posing and literacy activities ("reading the world and the word") in group dialogue that leads to action.

The strength of the coming chapters, then, lies in the diverse levels and locales in which Souto-Manning practices culture circles and reflects on the lessons of practice. The reinvention of Freire's method requires the *praxis* demonstrated in this book—reflective practice, practice based on theory, theory tested in practice. Souto-Manning's classrooms, then, are not only valuable to read about but also are sites worthy of visits, so that educators who dream of a more just world may view moments of that dream coming to life.

Introduction

Paulo Freire facilitates our attempt to conceptualize a democratic form of teaching...Freire has taught us that by using this information teachers identify "generative words and themes" that signify the most important subject matter for an emancipatory curriculum. Contrary to the belief of some critics of our critical pedagogical position, this subject matter is not simply passed uncritically along to our students...As Freire puts it, the subject matter is "problem-posed," that is, students and teachers reflect on the lives they lead asking questions of meaning and value...[which] leads to transformative action.

Kincheloe & Steinberg (1998, p. 20)

Paulo Freire's work, including his treatise *Pedagogy of the Oppressed* (1970), inspired many to embrace critical pedagogy. While *Pedagogy of the Oppressed* was situated within the context of Brazilian education, it shed light onto many contexts. Having taught in Pernambuco, Brazil, and attended workshops with Freire, critical pedagogy has long been a reality for me. I had lived it as a teacher in Brazil and continued to employ it as I immigrated to the United States. As proposed by Freire, I sought to recreate his pedagogy (Freire, 1998) in a new context. Nevertheless, some core aspects remained constant as addressed by the passage above authored by Joe Kincheloe and Shirley Steinberg (1998), even as culture circles crossed linguistic, cultural, contextual and socioeconomic borders.

Considering the dearth of information regarding culture circles in action despite its long history (c.f. Freire, 1959), in this book, I draw on my experience as a former teacher and current teacher educator. I share how I employed Freirean culture circles in three contexts: (1) primary grades; (2) pre-service teacher education; and (3) in-service teacher education in the United States. In addition, I describe a culture circle within the context of an adult literacy program in Northeastern Brazil. I do so in hopes of making this process clearer, more real and applicable in the fields of teaching and teacher education. In providing windows into how culture circles work across various contexts, I attend to their transformational power while addressing criticisms of critical pedagogy.

Freirean culture circles employ a generative approach to education, honoring participants' background experiences and knowledge. A generative approach works on the assumption that actions cannot be separated from the context in which they take place (Wertsch, 1991). For example, if we consider in-service trainings according to this approach, when the teacher arrives at the professional development site, he/she already has knowledge of his/her own language and everyday world. The teacher is the subject of his/her own learning (Freire, 1982). In this kind of professional development, each teacher investigates and engages in inquiry employing problem-posing, critical dialogue and problem solving. Learning takes place collectively and is directly linked to the shared experience, happening most effectively within critical, authentic dialogue (Freire, 1970; Vygotsky, 1978). Finally, democratic, reflective, and transformative practices are not spontaneous; they require continuous inquiry and research. There is much planning, yet the educator must know how to critically take advantage of teachable moments and engage students from multiple backgrounds and abilities in meaningful learning experiences.

Explaining the multiple components of culture circles and offering situated representations of change at the personal and social levels, I provide everyday examples from an elementary school classroom, pre-service teacher training in a public research university, and in-service professional development in the United States. In doing so, I strive to make culture circles more accessible to those seeking to embrace equity and democracy through everyday educational practices (Freire, 1967) while challenging issues such as the "sorting mechanism" of schools which continue to serve as an apparatus for the reproduction of a socially unjust system (Freire, 1992).

According to William Ayers (2001):

> There are still worlds to change—including specific, individual worlds, one by one—and classrooms can be places of possibility and transformation for youngsters, certainly, but also for teachers. Teaching can still do world-changing work. (p. 8)

I hope you enjoy reading this book, which is filled with theory-informed examples of how culture circles work across educational contexts (Chapters 3 through 7) and can result in real transformation. By reading it, you will have the basic tools and ideas to recreate Freirean culture circles in your own contexts, embracing transformative and democratic education (Freire, 1995). I hope this book will be a useful resource for those who are seeking to learn more about critical pedagogy across educational contexts and about Freire's culture circles, issues of social justice, teaching for equity, multicultural education, and curriculum/teaching methods.

Part I:

Culture Circles and Critical Pedagogy

CHAPTER 1

Culture Circles and Critical Pedagogy

No one constructs a serious democracy...without...radically changing the societal structures, reorienting the politics of production and development, reinventing power, doing justice to everyone, and abolishing the unjust and immoral gains of the all-powerful...The exercise of this democratic disposition in a truly open school...must first approach the authoritarian tendency, racist or machista...such as the denial of democracy, or freedoms, and of the rights of those who are different, as the denial of a necessary humanism.

Freire (1998, pp. 66-67)

One day, back in the 1990s, Paulo Freire (1921-1997) stood on the front steps of the Pernambuco state museum (Museu do Estado) in Recife and declared that the beauty of education is that it cannot do everything by itself, yet without it all other things cannot be done. Many have said that education does not promote transformation or that it has failed to do so. Freire, however, believed that education was a means, a tool for transformation.

This book is about the kind of education that lays out the foundation and process for transformation in schools and beyond. It is about applying critical pedagogy through Freirean culture circles across time and space. Despite the fact that Freirean culture circles were a reality in 1960s Brazil (Freire, 1959) such a pedagogical approach has resisted the test of time and geographic boundaries. In this book I explore the power and possibilities of Freirean culture circles in teaching and teacher education, from early education to in-service professional development, in Brazil and in the United States.

Political Nature of Education

According to Freire, education is inherently political. It should serve as a starting point and not as an end in itself. Freire himself proposed that education should encompass reading words and worlds. By becoming educated, individuals should be able to not only read the words printed on a page, but to solve mathematical equations and locate geographic regions and borders on a map. They should also be able to read the worlds around them, to contest mathematical and financial inequalities, and to reenvision their locations and challenge boundaries in society. To become educated in such a fashion, to learn how to read the world, to problematize it and to transform it, critical pedagogy is necessary.

According to Joe Kincheloe (2005), "proponents of critical pedagogy understand that every dimension of schooling and every form of educational practice are politically contested spaces" (p. 2). Whether challenging curricula, administrative decisions, or assumptions about diverse learners, critical educators' work is never done. Affecting educational settings and promoting transformative education requires the ability to communicate through conflict and consider multiple perspectives, breaking down barriers to social change. This is part of the problem-posing education advocated by Paulo Freire.

According to Lilia Bartolomé (1996):

> Teachers working toward political clarity understand that they can either maintain the status quo, or they can work to transform the sociocultural reality at the classroom and school level so that the culture at this micro-level does not reflect macro-level inequalities... (p. 235).

Freire proposed that through dialogue, individuals could reframe education as a problem-posing process, problematizing issues as opposed to seeking clear-cut solutions. Fennimore (2000) wrote that "Educators never 'just talk.' The language environment of any school or other educational institution serves as a dynamic platform for powerful attitudes and behaviors" (p. 4). Thus, it is very important to pay close attention to language, as language can be conceived as action, as behavior that makes things happen (Fennimore, 2008).

The very premise of Freirean education, problem-posing education, promotes the problematization of injustices and inequalities, contesting unfair realities. Taking a critical approach to analyzing language in use, Chouliaraki and Fairclough (1999) explained the process of colonization and appropriation through language. They posited that if language is accepted and not contested, it becomes part of an individual's repertoire and has the potential to colonize that person. For example, if individual people accept unequal and unfair access in educational settings, they are then colonized by such unfair realities. On the other hand, by problematizing, contesting language and concepts within specific contexts and taking sociohistorical and cultural issues into account, one gains the power to appropriate language, and utilize it to promote change. Contesting the status quo (or what *is* as defined by the dominant culture) becomes very important as one seeks to uncover the historicity of certain issues (such as socioeconomically and racially unequal access to schooling). Through language appropriation, individuals (whether five-year-old children or adults who've been teaching for over a dozen years) acquire the necessary tools for transformation.

Such language appropriation happens via a critical process which takes place in Freirean culture circles. Culture circles start from the very issues which affect participants' everyday lives. Generative themes, which are common experiences across participants' lives or relevant to participants' realities, serve as starting points to problem posing. As problems are posed, participants engage in dialogue, considering a multitude of perspectives, and seek to move towards problem solving. As the group engages in collective problem solving, it charts a course for action at the personal and/or societal levels.

As Freire (1998) proposed, the critical educational process is not about importing his pedagogy, but about recreating the process across contexts with regard to the specific cultures and histories of each community in which it takes place. Accordingly, I seek to illustrate some of the commonalities and differences of culture circles across contexts. In the studies portrayed within the chapters of Part II of this book, I convey the contemporary use of Freirean culture circles. While each of these culture circles has its own particularities and peculiarities, they all operate within a critical pedagogy paradigm.

Critical Pedagogy

Critical pedagogy is an educational process which situates schools within societies and considers structural forces which influence and shape schools. Critical pedagogy challenges the concept and idea of "culture-free" learning (Grant & Sleeter, 1996). It acknowledges that all learning is influenced by cultural differences and by the context in which it takes place (Freire, 1970; Ladson-Billings, 1994; Nieto, 1999). Furthermore, critical pedagogy sees all knowledge as built upon socioculturally and historically situated bodies of knowledge (Banks, 2004; Gutiérrez, 2008; Vygotsky, 1978).

Thus, teachers employing critical pedagogy in their own settings consider the multitude of cultures that make up the classroom, community, and society. They take into consideration the cultural nature of human development (Rogoff, 2003) as well as the cultural nature of knowledge per se. For example, while many believe that facts are absolute, they may vary widely across frontiers. In the United States, children are taught that the Wright brothers were the first to fly. In Brazil, students learn that Santos Dumont was the first to fly. Students in some countries (such as the U.S.) learn that America comprises two continents (North America and South America) while others (such as Brazil) learn that America is one continent. So, as it is quickly (and rather simplistically) identified here, knowledge is not always culture-free. Hence there is a need to teach individuals, rather than a curriculum. Teaching a curriculum without considering stu-

who decides?

dents' individually and culturally shaped backgrounds would be akin to considering that they come to schools and classrooms as blank slates or as empty banks into which teachers are to deposit knowledge.

The very premise of critical pedagogy seeks to move away from the model of education that is based on transmission of knowledge to students' brains like money into banks. Paulo Freire himself contested this idea and practice so common in classrooms throughout the world, labeling it the banking concept of education (Freire, 1970). Learning is co-constructed through social interactions. Hence, critical educators realize students enter classrooms and schools with specific bodies of knowledge that are socioculturally and historically located. Critical pedagogues propose that it is important to assess each student's historicity and build upon the wonderful backgrounds, legacies, skills, and knowledges students bring with them to the classroom. For example, I saw that as children in Recife, Brazil, entered public school classrooms, many of them knew street mathematics (Freire, 1998) since they had been selling goods at stop lights and could rapidly calculate change. In this case, a critical educator may capitalize on these mathematical skills, building upon students' strengths and bodies of knowledge.

Critical pedagogy values the concept of historicity individually as well as collectively. Individually, critical pedagogy values and builds upon previous experiences one may have had. Collectively, it considers conditions which shaped certain shared situations. Freire and Macedo (1987) proposed that worlds and words are socially and historically located. As such, to be able to challenge and change their worlds, individuals need to start reading the history of their worlds in order to name the issues oppressing them. How does this happen? What causes this situation? Such questions can get at the real issues, assessing larger structural forces that shape individual lives. In this way, individuals have not only to problematize their locations, but to move away from those locations by problematizing and seeking to look into the forces and structures that historically framed any specific oppressive situation. For example, in *Education for Democracy*

(Souto-Manning, 2007), I documented the ways in which adult participants in Freirean culture circles started questioning issues that were deeply historical, such as unequal gender pay for equal work. This had been shaped partly by the historical expectation that males would be breadwinners and conversely by the relatively recent phenomenon of women working outside of the home full-time on a large scale. Considering historical issues did not serve to justify and to foster complacency, but to help students understand the complexities involved and to be better prepared to engage in transformative action.

Many educators and researchers (Freire, 1970; Giroux, 1997; Kincheloe, 2005; McLaren, 2000) have defined central aspects of critical pedagogy. These aspects were compiled by Joe Kincheloe (2005) and are listed below:

1. Grounded in a social and educational vision of justice, equality, and the belief that education is inherently political;
2. Dedicated to the alleviation of human suffering, takes first-hand knowledge into consideration, prevents students from being blamed for failing;
3. Based on generative themes (reading the word and the world in the process of problem posing);
4. Positions teachers as researchers, as learners. Authority is dialectical; focuses on facilitation and problem posing.

First, *critical pedagogy is grounded in a social and educational vision of justice, equality, and the belief that education is inherently political.* Critical pedagogy challenges the belief of education as neutral. By helping students become critical thinkers, education has the potential to be transformative. I am not proposing that education is a cure for all ailments of the world, but that critical education has the potential to make individuals aware of injustices as they start reading words and worlds. Critical pedagogy recognizes that language and educational practices have the power to serve as sites for colonization (if banking education is the norm and students are expected to espouse a specific set of beliefs) or for appropriation and transformation (if perspectives are considered and become tools for recognizing and challenging the status quo). By being grounded in the concepts of justice and equality, critical pedagogy seeks to provide the tools for individuals to be able to recognize their oppressions instead of accepting them as predeterminations. Recognizing oppression is, after all, the first step towards change.

Second, *critical pedagogy is dedicated to the alleviation of human suffering, takes first-hand knowledge into consideration, and prevents students from being blamed for failing.* Critical pedagogy is not about causing the rich to become richer, but about alleviating oppressive situations, power over, and recurring oppression. Because critical pedagogy recognizes that knowledge is not culture-free (Grant & Sleeter, 1996), it takes first-hand knowledge into consideration as a legitimate source. After all, much of what we know as history has been written from a White, male perspective (Boxer, 1998). Often, perspectives of women and people of color have been historically excluded from books. Nevertheless, our schools educate more and more females and students of color. As such, critical pedagogy prevents students from being blamed for failing. It does not buy into the "s/he cannot learn" mantra that is so widely muttered in schools. It directly challenges the kind of educational accountability sponsored by legislation and programs such as *No Child Left Behind*. Measuring student performance and testing does not do anything to alleviate human suffering and it blames students for failing. Critical pedagogy poses that if students are not learning, it is because there are larger issues shaping the situation (e.g., racial inequity, what counts in the classroom, etc.).

Third, *critical pedagogy is based on generative themes* (reading the word and the world in the process of problem posing). Generative themes are generated from the experiences of students, their families, and communities. To be able to access these generative themes, teachers must embrace the fluidity of the roles of teacher and learner (Freire, 1970). Only by blurring these roles can teachers truly engage in accessing these generative themes. Such an action "allows us to transform whatever sense of certainty and cultural superiority we might bring to school into a genuine search for the history and meaning behind specific practices" (Ayers, 2001, p. 77).

Finally, teachers position themselves as ethnographers, learning from observation, coding the information collected, and employing learnings in their new plans. This approach to teaching affirms diversities and considers students' perspectives. By starting with not only what students know, but with the issues that are truly important in their out-of-school lives, teachers have a better chance to engage all students in naming the issues and engaging in problem-posing education. In this process, authority is dialectically negotiated as teachers assume the role of facilitators and focus on problem posing as they seek to engage in critical education (Kincheloe & Steinberg, 1998).

Critical pedagogy advocates that "[m]aking the classroom a democratic setting where everyone feels a responsibility to contribute is a central goal of transformative pedagogy" (hooks, 1994, p. 39). Culture circles are sites in which individuals learn to read words and worlds while engaging in "honest confrontation, and dialogue" (p. 106).

Historical Accounts of Culture Circles

Culture circles were first conceptualized by Paulo Freire in the 1950s. While there are various accounts of how long it took participants to become literate and how many were touched by such pedagogical innovation, the power of culture circles has been conveyed by multiple studies (Mashayekh, 1974; Brown, 1975; Pelandré, 2002) over time.

Freire initiated the practice of culture circles in Brazil in the early 1960s (Tennant, 1995) when developing his adult literacy method. Culture circles were central to Freire's doctoral dissertation on *Educação e Atualidade Brasileira* (Education and Contemporary Brazil) at the Escola de Belas Artes de Pernambuco, Universidade de Recife in 1959, currently the Universidade Federal de Pernambuco. During the time in which Freire developed the idea behind the circles, he first worked with two students who learned how to read in a period of between two and three months as he reported in the video *Paulo Freire*

(Instituto Paulo Freire et al., n.d.). He had never properly implemented the circles as he had conceived them. The opportunity to do so came with the Movimento de Cultura Popular or MCP (Popular Culture Movement or PCM) in the state of Pernambuco. While Freire first implemented culture circles in Recife, Brazil, he expanded his work in the city of Angicos, Rio Grande do Norte, Brazil. Freire took advantage of a great offer from the city of Angicos to implement the literacy method he proposed in his dissertation. But it did not last long.

According to Mashayekh (1974), Freire taught 300 people how to read and write in three months. Elias (1994) claimed that the people of Angicos became literate in 45 days. Brown recounted that Freire's literacy method took place in 30 hours (1975; 1978). More recently, Pelandré (2002), in a book published by the Paulo Freire Institute, listed 40 hours as the requisite time. Despite the inconsistencies of these accounts, it is clear that the program worked extremely well, yet it is uncertain as to the exact amount of time it took.

> The success of the Angicos project was such that Freire was invited by his friend, Paulo de Tarso, newly appointed minister of education in the populist government of President João Goulart (1961-4), to become the director of the Brazilian National Literacy Program...In that capacity Freire drew plans for 20,000 culture circles to involve two million people by 1964, extending the pattern of literacy work throughout the country...In a period of three or four months, Freire and his team worked with thousands of illiterate workers. (de Figueiredo-Cowen & Gestaldo, 1995, p. 65)

In 1964, a year after the implementation of culture circles in Angicos, the military, assisted, organized, and funded by the United States government (Azevedo, Domeneci, Amaral, Tendler, Viana, Arbex Jr., et al., 2004; Coben, 1998) forcefully overtook the elected Brazilian government. A military dictatorship was established and initially supported by the Kennedy government. In 1964, Freire's program was extinguished within 14 days of the coup d'etat. His culture circles had become so powerful that they came to be seen as a threat to the military government. Thus Freire's culture circles were dismantled soon after the coup d'etat.

After the military coup of April 1964, the Brazilian popular educator Paulo Freire was arrested, imprisoned, and eventually forced into exile. Government authorities were reacting to Freire's successes in mounting massive literacy campaigns among illiterate adults. Freire's Popular Culture Movement (PCM) had been expanding to include 20,000 "Culture Circles," each serving 25 to 30 rural and urban slum residents who were working to build both their literacy skills and an awareness of their collective ability to generate change in their community. (Cummins & Sayers, 1995, p. 336)

Considered an anti-American and a communist (as a member of the Brazilian Communist Party, PCB), Freire was arrested and put in jail for 70 days in Recife (Gadotti, 1994). He was then exiled to Bolivia, where he went without his wife Elza and their five children. The following year, Freire went to Chile, where he re-joined his family and resumed his critical literacy programs. At this time however, culture circles were not a reality in Brazil. From Chile to the United States to Europe to various countries in Africa, Freire continued to develop his work as reported in *Pedagogy in Process: Letters to Guinea-Bissau* (1978). In Chile, "Freire's system became an official program of the government, and Chile was recognized by UNESCO as one of the five nations most effective in overcoming illiteracy" (Roberts, 2000, p. 83).

In the 1980s, Freire returned to Brazil. Following a two-year transition, democracy was finally re-established in Brazil in 1986. In that same year, Miguel Arraes, who had been exiled for his revolutionary ideas and for sponsoring culture circles, was elected the governor of Pernambuco in an emotionally charged campaign (Araújo, 1991). He represented the return to a time before the dictatorship. Arraes was elected and re-established culture circles in Pernambuco, making them the model for adult literacy programs in the state. Culture circles have contributed to the development of agency by thousands of people since their inception in the 1960s (Freire, 2000). Adult literacy programs based on Freire's culture circles are functioning throughout Brazil, from Pernambuco (Secretaria de Educação e Esportes, Governo do Estado de Pernambuco, 1997) in Northeastern Brazil to Rio Grande do Sul (Brandão, 2001), the southern-most Brazilian state.

Culture Circles: Reading Words and Worlds

According to Paulo Freire (1985) literacy should be a tool for personal transformation and social change, and it can only be so if what students are learning is directly related to their lives. Education and knowledge have value only if they help people free themselves from oppressive social conditions (Freire, 2000), thereby providing the tools for social change. Freire advocated that education includes reading words and worlds, texts and contexts. But, how do we accomplish this? At the same time that Freire proposed the necessity of considering power and/in society as the process of education, he also stated that he did not want his pedagogy to be generically imported but rather recreated. In this book, I present the power and possibilities of culture circle principles applied across contexts. While I present situated representations of one way of engaging students in reading words and worlds, it is certainly not the only one.

In culture circles, Freire (2000) emphasized that prior experiences and community concerns of students are the starting points in teaching reading and writing. Schooling was necessary not only to learn the letters of the alphabet, but also to know each person, the way they expressed themselves, how people are different, their different interests, and finding ways to approach a problem. Participants were not classified as illiterate, but as "literants" (literacy learners). Each one of them brought knowledge regarding themselves/their worlds. Teachers facilitated the entrance of learners into the literate world. Freire stressed the use of literacy development for personal transformation and personal action (Huerta-Macias, 1993). "Freire's aim was never to make people function better within any given system. Instead, he wanted them to become aware of injustices and to act in order to change them" (Finger & Asún, 2001, p. 86).

Culture circles are grounded on the belief that "...no educational experience takes place in a vacuum, only in a real context—historical, economic, political, and not necessarily identical to any other context" (Freire, 1985, p. 12). Throughout this book, I highlight the pedagogies which apply across contexts and how these concepts came to life in different and context-specific ways.

Overall, culture circles are based on two basic tenets: the political nature of education (Feitosa, 1999a; Freire, 1985) and dialogue in the process of educating. These tenets take place within the context in which the learners live, as their problems are analyzed critically and politically, and dialogue is used as a way to progressively overcome and find solutions to those problems. Dialogue became such a central concept for Freire that, in the 1980s, he began authoring books in dialogue format as his method advocated (Instituto Paulo Freire, Gadotti, & Antunes, n.d.).

Culture circles aim to promote *conscientização* (Freire, 1970). According to Apple, Gandin, and Hypolito (2001), "in concrete terms, his methods of 'conscientization' with adults in literacy programmes was basically constituted by a process of coding/decoding linguistic and social meanings, organized through a number of steps" (p. 131). The first step is to generate themes from the community in which students live. The generative themes are socially and culturally relevant to individuals and communities. After the generation of themes, they are employed in dialogues in the circles. Specific "steps are taken to achieve the process of reading...[which] consist of a process of decoding written words...from a coded existential situation. This connection to the real existential situation is...crucial...enabling students...to use...knowledge to reconstruct their lives" (p. 132).

Although there may be a number of steps, there is no predetermined formula for the implementation of culture circles. Culture circles intend to eliminate the dichotomy between theory and practice often present in the traditional schooling environment as practice depends on theory and theory depends on practice in the implementation, development, and maintenance of culture circles.

There are common aspects in all culture circles. These are not pre-scriptive, and need to be re-created as new instances occur and culture circles are implemented in different contexts across time and space. These common aspects are: generative themes (which include thematic investigation and codification), problem posing, dialogue, and problem solving leading to action. They come to life differently and are constantly being renegotiated. In the beginning, thematic investigations lead to generative themes. These involve the exploration and documentation of the social, cultural, and linguistic contexts of the learners. A thematic investigation is initially done by the facilitator who takes on the role of an ethnographer, learning about the culture of the learners' communities. Common and recursive phenomena are then coded into generative themes. As time goes by and participants take more ownership of the process, this may become a task undertaken by the group. An example of this shift is presented in Chapter 4. These generative themes are then codified into words, drawings, vignettes, or other representational formats. The artifact resulting from the codification represents the very issues experienced by the participants without exposing the individual(s) experiencing the situation. Because it is often a representation of a phenomenon commonly experienced by several participants, it represents a collective experience which includes details of many situated representations as opposed to details of one case only. Participants then engage in problem posing, seeking to do away with innocent and simplistic views of the world or any specific situation, looking critically at, and transforming the situation in place. Transformation happens through dialogue and problem solving in a cyclical and recursive process which leads to transformative action. Those common aspects are illustrated as the critical cycle in Figure 1.1.

In establishing a democratic culture circle, Ira Shor (1990) asserted that the first task of the critical educator is to deconstruct authoritarian modes of discourse in conventional classrooms. In culture circles, students' experiences are invited, valued, and central to the construction of meaning. This is not a simple process, however. According to Freire (1987), "a progressive position requires democratic practice where authority never becomes authoritarianism, and where authority is never so reduced that it disappears in a climate of irresponsibility and license" (p. 212). As you will see in Part II of this book, there is neither a simple definition of culture circles nor a formula for implementing them. An educator must dare to blur teacher and learner roles, positioning himself/herself vulnerably yet responsibly.

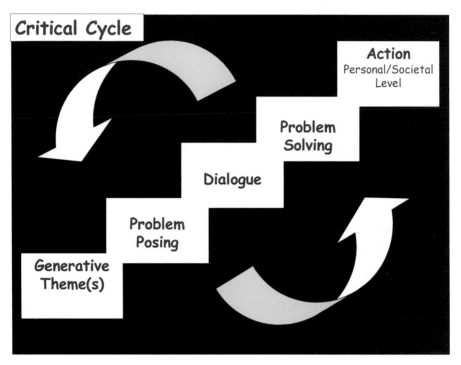

Figure 1.1. Critical cycle (Souto-Manning, 2007).

Culture circles are spaces to seize conflicts as opportunities for learning. Freire (1997) proposed the use of problematization or the technique of problem posing to initiate dialogue. According to Moacir Gadotti (Instituto Paulo Freire et al., n.d.), we only learn what is meaningful, otherwise we forget. Taking the students' experiences as central to the literacy process respects their discourses and cultures while making learning memorable and relevant. The student is therefore the protagonist in the culture circles, in the literacy process.

For example, participants of a culture circle I observed in Bezerros, Pernambuco, Brazil, were problematizing their own location in society in terms of gender (Souto-Manning, 2009b). The women were sharing their experiences of not being able to attend school beyond the elementary years. Although this is a historical reality in Bezerros, it is based on a set of patriarchal beliefs and was explained in terms of community morals; one participant said that "girls have to stay home and help their mothers." Through dialogue, participants in the culture circle I observed ultimately challenged this set of beliefs. They challenged gendered education as a predetermined fact and, seeing the issue as a barrier to the advancement of women, posed it as a problem, dialogued, and negotiated some possible solutions and responses to society at large. They plotted actions they could implement on a personal level to make sure their own daughters would not become victims of the structure in place. One of the solutions was to organize groups of girls who would walk together to the schools that were farther from where they lived so they would not become "badly spoken of" for walking alone, as one of them articulated. As seen in this example, knowledge is based on what individuals and/or groups believe and what has happened in the past, and it is co-constructed in conversations (Ochs & Capps, 2001), in dialogue (Freire, 1970), by challenging sociocultural assumptions.

The Freirean curriculum (Heaney, 1989) or method (Feitosa, 1999b) is based on the principle that experience and enacted elements inform curriculum design (Marsh & Willis, 1999). The curriculum of study comes directly from the learners who are participants in their own learning (Freire, 1997). There are no traditional textbooks adopted in these circles. The process of constructing and working with the curriculum in culture circles is complex because it is "literally hand-made from the social fabrics of the students' lives" (Salvio, 1998, p. 69). Such aspects of the curriculum in the culture circles and the seamless engagement of theory and practice, as proposed by Freire, serve to dispel the criticism that critical pedagogy theorists such as Freire could do more to recognize the realities of educational contexts, instead of remaining at the theoretical level (Gore, 1993).

Prior to implementing the culture circles, teachers and/or coordinators learn from the community in which the circle will be implemented. Engaging in what Freire referred to as field vocabulary research, they collect words and phrases and observe and record common situations in that particular community. From what could be called *corpus analysis* (Stubbs, 1996), these teachers come up with a word list according to occurrence and relevance. A thematic list is also generated using a similar process. These words and themes relevant to the community become the core of the circles. These lists are then codified into pictures or other visual representations. Consequently, participants are able to engage in deeper dialogue, as the specific method focuses on their strengths and on the knowledge that emerged from their own universe, as opposed to accentuating their limited literacy skills with unfamiliar terms and experiences. This is done as students "begin to read and write,...[and] come to understand that reading and writing are not neutral acts; rather, they are linked to cultural practices that make political, epistemic, and moral claims on our lives" (Stubbs, 1996, p. 69).

Culture circles initially aimed to promote the social competence of adults of low SES (Secretaria de Educação e Esportes, Governo do Estado de Pernambuco, 1997), but have proven to be useful and powerful across time and space with any population that experiences oppression or power over (e.g., Souto-Manning, 2009b). The work world and other everyday issues are systematized and become part of the circles. Their pedagogical intent is to democratize education and culture.

Towards Dialogical, Political, Critical Spaces

Through the exploration of relevant issues and themes, culture circle participants engage in inquiry, questioning, and charting a course of action. As they problematize themes and issues, old knowledge and assumptions collide with new knowledge. Participants can then construct their own knowledge in a critical manner. This happens as participants share their experiences and perspectives and listen to other perspectives as alternatives, as multiple angles or explanations.

As Paulo Freire (Instituto Paulo Freire, n.d.) wrote (Figure 1.2), "It is as impossible to negate the political nature of the educational proc-

ess as [it is] to negate the educational character of the political act..."
(trans. by author).

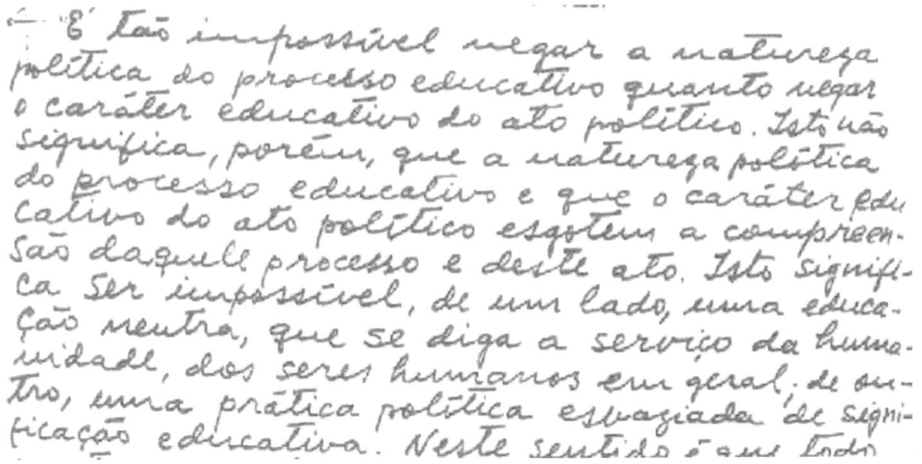

É tão impossível negar a natureza política do processo educativo quanto negar o caráter educativo do ato político. Isto não significa, porém, que a natureza política do processo educativo e que o caráter educativo do ato político esgotem a compreensão daquele processo e deste ato. Isto significa ser impossível, de um lado, uma educação neutra, que se diga a serviço da humanidade, dos seres humanos em geral; de outro, uma prática política esvaziada de significação educativa. Neste sentido é que...

Figure 1.2. Freire's notes.

In situated examples of circles analyzed in Part II of this book, participants engaged in problematizing issues such as standardized testing, developmentally appropriate practice, Englishes, and monthly minimum-wage salaries, situations about which participants initially believed they could do little to change. Through problematizing and dialoguing about some of the issues involved, they collectively designed a plan of action. Through culture circles, literants in Brazil, young children in U.S. public schools, pre-service teachers in an American research university, and early childhood teachers in the U.S. were becoming aware of tools they could use (problem posing, dialogue, and problem solving) to question the status quo and to start believing in and even negotiating change. Over several meetings, across settings and languages, they repeatedly engaged in the process of naming, problematizing, and renaming everyday issues (see Figure 1.3) intrinsic to their lives. Such a process is cyclical, recursive, critical and formative.

As subjects of their own learning, participants brought authentic issues to the circles and engaged in meaningful learning experiences, applicable to their everyday lives, gaining ownership of their learning. They made clear connections between what they lived and what they learned together.

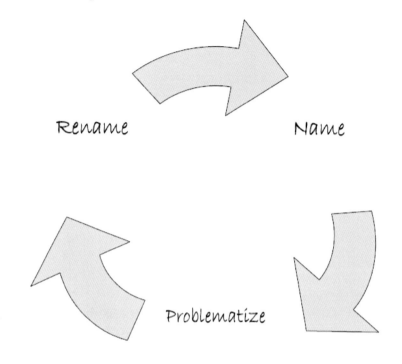

Rename   Name

Problematize

Figure 1.3.   Inner workings of critical discursive turns (Souto-Manning, 2009b).

Critically Reading Discourses and Identities

As mentioned early in this chapter, Freire's culture circles, which were conceived in the 1950s, already employed a definition of literacy that challenged and departed from what has traditionally been conceived as literacy. The "traditional meaning of the word 'literacy'—the ability to read and write—appears innocent and obvious. But it is no such thing. Literacy as 'the ability to write and read' situates literacy in the individual person, rather than in society" (Gee, 1996, p. 22). Applying sociocultural theory (Vygotsky, 1978) to the definition of literacy, Freire wrote that "[l]iteracy is best understood as a myriad of [communication] forms and cultural competencies that construct and make available the various relations and experiences that exist between learners and the world" (Freire & Macedo, 1989, p. 10). Paulo Freire's conceptualization of literacy in the culture circles was crafted in terms of identities and discourses. He integrated oral and written styles of communication in his adult literacy programs. "Learning to *read* the word, emerged from purposeful discussion of generative words and codifications through the medium of the spoken word. Dialogue provides the bridge between oral and literate forms of interpreting, understanding, and transforming the world" (Roberts, 2000, p. 91).

An alternative definition of literacy is presented by Gee (1996), who defined literacy in terms of learning the school Discourse (with capital D). To him, Discourses are "ways of being in the world, or forms of life which integrate words, acts, values, beliefs, attitudes, and social identities, as well as gestures, glances, body positions and clothes" (Gee, 1996, p. 127). A Freirean conception of critical literacy is concerned with the development of a particular way of being and acting (Roberts, 2000). Gee stated that there can be no critique of a Discourse without learning because it is through the process of learning that meta-knowledge can be developed. Further, Gee argued that the goal of a strong literacy program should be a balance of acquisition and learning. This balance is part of what takes place in Freire's culture circles. However, Freire's definition of literacy has a more critical aim. Freire's definition of literacy includes rewriting the world or engaging in social action.

Both Freire (1970) and Gee (1996) have agreed that we cannot teach people new discourses merely by teaching them the rules, but rather by making them members of the group—by allowing them to be apprentices (Gee, 1996). Referring to a particular situated context, Freire and Macedo (1987) found that "[l]iteracy in the case of Nicaragua started to take place as soon as the people took their history into their own hands. Taking history into their own hands precedes taking up the alphabet. Anyone who takes history into his or her own hands can easily take up the alphabet" (p. 106). Assumptions and socially constructed knowledge are deconstructed. As one discourse is used to critique others, the assumption of right and wrong, standard and nonstandard discourse is hopefully challenged and subdued. Discourses are then couched in situated terms. The use of a particular discourse to critique others is the foundation for resistance to oppression and inequality (Delpit, 1995).

As Freire (1996) suggested, the world is in the making; the world isn't fixed (as a permanent and unchangeable reality) but is continuously being (re)configured and (re)constructed (Instituto Paulo Freire, n.d.). Identity is one way of naming the dense interconnections between the intimate and public venues of social practice. In Freire's (1996) culture circles, "a fundamental starting point is respect for the learner's cultural identity and the aspects of class that mark this identity: the learner's language, syntax, prosody, semantics, and informal knowledge, realized through the experiences the learner brings to school" (p. 127).

Practiced identities are constructs that can be defined by reference to several contexts of activity. The identity contexts proposed by Holland, Skinner, and Cain (2001) closely align with the steps taken in culture circles. In culture circles, from reading the world, one critically analyzes one's position in society, engages in problem solving through dialogue, and engages in social action or rewriting the world. In this way, literacy as defined by Freire is similar to Holland, Skinner, and Cain's definition of identity, which goes from embodying one's fixed social location to negotiating one's way into multiple cultural worlds as a knowledgeable and committed participant. Identity, therefore, surpasses the boundaries of cultural traditions, improvising and redescribing selves, and constructing novel cultural worlds (Holland, Skinner, & Cain, 2001).

Freire's definition of literacy included dialogue, which addresses "[o]ne of the most difficult tasks we face as human beings...communicating meaning across our individual differences, a task confounded immeasurably when we attempt to communicate across social lines, racial lines, cultural lines, or lines of unequal power" (Delpit, 1995, p. 66). According to Giroux (1987):

Central to Freire's approach to literacy is a dialectical relationship between human beings and the world, on the one hand, and language and transformative agency on the other. Within this perspective, literacy is not approached as merely a technical skill to be acquired, but as a necessary foundation for cultural action for freedom, a central aspect of what it means to be a self and socially constituted agent. Most importantly, literacy for Freire is inherently a political project in which men and women assert their right, a responsibility not only to read, understand and transform their own experiences, but also to reconfigure their relationship with wider society. (p. 7)

Freire's definition of literacy provided spaces for students to make "connections between their local, national, racial, cultural, and global identities" and view knowledge as socially constructed, as "continuously re-created, recycled, and shared by teachers and students alike" (Ladson-Billings, 1994, p. 25) as represented by Figure 1.3.

Reading This Book Together

Throughout this book, you have the opportunity to read about culture circles across contexts. Although each chapter in Part II presents a singular study, there are common characteristics across chapters. In Chapters 3 through 7, participants' interests and issues determined the curriculum taught. Teachers facilitated. Starting from themes inherent in the participants' lives is a very positive aspect of culture circles. The pedagogical intent of culture circles remains the same across contexts: to democratize education and culture. More than formation, critical pedagogy as applied in culture circles strives to promote the social competence of people within and across a community of practices, and improve their quality of life. These circles take place in many locations. Primarily, they take place wherever it is convenient for most of the members. Some of them take place in schools, clubs, syndicates/unions, and churches.

Across contexts, specific and technical skills are embraced, but the process reigns over content since no one person is held as the sole expert. The rich experience of each of the individuals is respected and valued in the circle. There isn't a member who doesn't know anything; every person has important life experiences to share. These experiences become the themes for the meetings. Participants are not classified as receptacles of knowledge, but as active agents who collectively produce, construct and deconstruct multiple bodies of knowledge. Each one of them brings knowledge, explanations, ideas regarding themselves and their worlds. They bring and share their dreams, wishes, fears, questions, doubts, and frustrations; these are starting points for educational and social action. The curricula emanate from the community—the prayers, the syndicates, the social behavior of the group—nothing escapes the attention of the critical educators who facilitate the process.

In these studies, teachers know and believe that dialogue is the essential condition of their work—the teacher's job is to coordinate and to facilitate, but never to influence or impose. These teachers see dialogue as integral to the process rather than an accessory or technique. As you read the chapters in Part II of this book, I invite you to observe the role of the teachers/facilitators. It is at times difficult to notice their contributions, as they were meant to move the dialogue forward and not to dominate or control what happened. You will notice that such educators "understand that even as they teach, they will also be taught; even as they help others develop, they will themselves change and grow" (Ayers, 2001, p. 77). The teacher-facilitator takes a vulnerable and risky position as he/she negotiates the dance of dynamically belonging in two (or more) categories at once—a messy yet real and necessary process.

After exploring the critical cycle of culture circles (Chapter 2), in Part II (Chapters 3-7), I invite you to take a journey through multiple culture circles and pay attention to the process across contexts. I invite you to pay attention to how the teachers/facilitators problematize their roles as they invite women and men, boys and girls to recognize their contributions and knowledges as worthy and come to understand a world in which there is no absolute knowledge (Harding, 1986), but a world in which situated knowledges (Hill Collins, 1990) are celebrated!

CHAPTER 2

The Critical Cycle

Students, as they are increasingly posed with problems relating to themselves in the world and with the world, will feel increasingly challenged and obliged to respond to that challenge. Because they apprehend the challenge as interrelated to other problems within a total context, not as a theoretical question, the resulting comprehension tends to be increasingly critical and thus constantly less alienated. Their response to the challenge evokes new challenges, followed by new understandings; and gradually the students come to regard themselves as committed.

Freire (2000, p. 81)

Often (and in multiple locations) students have the idea that classes are something they have to sit through and accordingly reflect contents which are not directly applicable to their everyday realities. Despite treatises such as Freire's *Pedagogy of the Oppressed* (1970) and Gloria Ladson-Billings' *The Dreamkeepers: Successful Teachers of African American Children* (1994), there is still an artificial division between in- and out-of-school literacies (Hull & Schultz, 2000). Long ago, American philosopher and educator John Dewey challenged this disconnect by stating that "Education is not a preparation for life; education is life itself." Despite the wisdom conveyed in Dewey's quote, many classroom practices today still strive to prepare students for future success, focusing on readiness (Graue, 2006). In this book, I share a generative and transformative approach to education which honors students' background experiences and knowledges. In teacher education, this transformative approach considers what teachers are already doing in their classrooms and builds upon promising practices while challenging oppressive structures.

In this chapter, I outline the recursive and cyclical phases (which can only be artificially and analytically pulled apart) of the critical cycle which characterizes culture circles in teaching and teacher education. Such a process is generative because themes discussed and issues addressed are generated directly from the students' experiences.

Culture circles are grounded on Freirean pedagogy (Freire, 1970). In these circles, social interaction mediates the learning process (Berk & Winsler, 1995). They function according to the belief that texts and contexts shape each other dynamically and symbiotically. Thus, actions cannot be considered apart from their sociocultural, historical, and interactional contexts (Wertsch, 1991). According to this approach:

- when the student arrives in the school or classroom, he/she already has knowledge of his/her own language and everyday world;
- the student is the subject of his/her own learning. In this kind of educational setting, each student investigates and engages in inquiry employing problem posing, critical dialogue and problem solving; *Responsibility*
- conflict is the basis for learning. When old knowledge and new knowledge conflict, participants ask questions and dialogue, critically (de)constructing their own bodies of knowledge;
- learning is directly linked to the collective experience and happens most effectively within a collective dialogue;
- culturally revelant pedagogy (Ladson-Billings, 1996) is not spontaneous; it requires continuous inquiry and research. There is much planning, yet the teacher/facilitator (or Freire's term *co-*

appreciative / anti-deficit approach

ordinator) must know how to critically take advantage of teachable moments and engage students/participants from multiple backgrounds and communities in meaningful learning experiences (Freire, 1970).

The Pedagogy of Culture Circles

As highlighted in Chapter 1, culture circles were conceptualized by Paulo Freire in the 1950s. They were conceptualized as pedagogical spaces sponsoring and supporting a liberatory adult-literacy education program first described in Freire's doctoral dissertation, *Educação e Atualidade Brasileira* (1959). In these circles, students learned how to read letters and the world, write words and their own histories (Feitosa, 1999b). These culture circles took real-life or relevant relationships provided or lived by the students to create generative themes. The participants provided their own experiences, which were presented as problems to the culture circle (Brown, 1978). Having had firsthand experience conducting Freirean culture circles, I learned that while it would be easiest to have students volunteer the most oppressive aspects of their lives in these settings, they are initially reluctant to do so. To create a community of learners based on trust and respect, I suggest that it is helpful for teachers to position themselves as ethnographers, studying the cultural practices within and across the communities learners inhabit. By documenting the most urgent struggles experienced by many of the participants of a culture circle and codifying those experiences in a generative theme (e.g., a case, story, photo, drawing, document), facilitators open up opportunities for students to name, problematize and deconstruct issues which are paramount in their lives.

According to Gadotti (Instituto Paulo Freire et al., n.d.), knowledge is not only historical, epistemological, and logical, it is also dialogical. Through dialogue, we build and change the world. Through dialogue, culture circle participants can challenge beliefs and realities commonly perceived as static. Collectively and dialogically, participants can challenge socioculturally and historically constructed oppressions such as gendered education. Through a variety of topics which are connected to their very lives, participants engage in posing problems, dialoguing, and deriving some possible solutions and responses in individual and societal realms.

Some of the topics brought to culture circles are complex and multi-layered—raced, gendered, and classed experiences and practices, for example. Exactly because of their complexities and histories, these are the kinds of issues to be addressed in culture circles. In referring to the power of culture circles, Angela Antunes (Instituto Paulo Freire, n.d.) highlighted the importance of problematizing the gendered and raced experiences of the participants in the culture circles, as these are at the root of much oppression. This pedagogical practice is not without its challenges, but it is necessary to engage in truly transformative and liberatory pedagogy.

The critical cycle inherent in culture circles has five phases: (1) generative themes, (2) problem posing, (3) dialogue, (4) problem solving, and (5) action. As illustrated by Figure 1.1 (Chapter 1), this approach is a recursive process. It is reflective in nature because it starts with data from participants' lives and aims to promote transformative action. Additionally, the critical cycle takes individual characteristics and interests under consideration as it is an applied approach to education in a very Deweyan sense. It is a process which refutes panoptical definitions of time, and is therefore not hurried. The process is as important as the topic being approached. The pedagogy of the culture circles is critical and meant to be continued over time across many meetings.

Culture circles employ what has been called Freirean methodology (Feitosa, 1999a; 1999b). Although Donaldo Macedo and Nita Freire (1998) have explicitly stated that:

> This fetish for method works insidiously against the ability to adhere to Freire's own pronouncement against importing and exporting methodology. In a long conversation Paulo had with Donaldo Macedo about this issue, he said: "Donaldo, I don't want to be imported or exported. It is impossible to export pedagogical practices without reinventing them. Please tell your fellow

American educators not to import me. Ask them to re-create and rewrite my ideas." (p. x).

In doing so, culture circles not only recognize the discourses of students, but allow students to learn from their own discourses, whether by employing themes present in the students' realities or by teaching from words that already figure in their vocabularies. Learning the school discourse (or Discourse, according to Gee, 1996) is paramount to success in education and schooling as traditionally (and currently) conceived.

In my own experience (Souto-Manning, 2007; 2009a; 2009b), when the literacy process goes beyond reading words to reading what is written between the lines in the realm of the world, generative themes which are significant to many participants are brought to the group to be problematized. While initially not exposing individuals, participants are then able to engage in the problematization of situations relevant to their everyday lives.

Within problematization or problem posing, there are five ground rules outlined by Freire in *Education: The practice of freedom* (1974/1976). He emphasized the following:

1. Learning/Knowing the linguistic universe of learners;
2. Choosing the words or themes from the linguistic universe learned—this selection is based on phonemic richness, rising level of difficulty, and pragmatics;
3. Creation of existential situations (situations typical to the lives of learners);
4. Elaboration of the curricular proposal (not a set curriculum); and
5. Deconstruction of generative words or themes.

While Freire stated that his method should not be exported or imported, much attention is given (in Part I of this book as well as in other publications) to the various steps, phases or components of his method. While this might initially signal potential conflict, I propose that Freire followed certain procedures which can be recreated across time and space. The exact curriculum, however, varies with each situated representation of this phenomenon (Dyson & Genishi, 2005)—

the transformative, critical pedagogy of culture circles. Freire gave the educator the freedom to engage in curricular practices without strict fidelity to implementation; to do what teachers do best—adapt, borrow, and re-create what will be most beneficial to individual students and/or groups of students in particular settings. One of the "most empowering [aspects of culture circles] was the way...Freire expanded the notion of literacy to include reading the world and writing the world as cultural agents and subjects rather than as objects of history...establishing a culture circle as a pedagogical space" (Steiner, Krank, McLaren, & Bahruth, 2000, p. 122).

The role of the teacher/facilitator in culture circles is extremely demanding, as he/she is constantly engaging in research as part of his/her teaching. It "requires constant reflection and criticity of one's own pedagogy" (p. 122). She/he is concurrently both a learner and a teacher. Corresponding with what Ellsworth (1992) suggested, that "a relation between teacher/student becomes voyeuristic when the voice of the pedagogue himself goes unexamined" (p. 104), in the circles, teachers reflect on their own practices and voices collectively. Each teacher participates in practice that promotes inclusion, engagement and empowerment of learners (Keesing-Styles, 2003). Thus teachers/facilitators use the very same framework for staff development, as they problematize, dialogue, problem-solve and prepare to engage in action in their own classrooms. After all, "[i]f a teacher is to be hopeful and optimistic in her teaching, she must take action—waiting cannot bring hope" (Ayers, 2001, p. 77).

In the circles, the seating arrangement breaks hierarchies set in traditional classrooms in which the teacher is the holder of knowledge and stands in front of the classroom while students face the teacher, from whom they are to learn. According to Kincheloe, Steinberg, Rodriguez, and Chennault (1998), the physical seating arrangement in circles is essential to employ dialogue and problem-posing education (Freire and Macedo, 1995). The seating arrangement in circles goes against the traditional banking concept of education, in which knowledge is deposited in students' heads. Circular seating is conducive to dialogue. It allows students to look at each other, see everyone, and value everyone's voices.

In such a setting, there is a need to problematize and redefine discourses, knowledges, curricula and learnings. The teacher does not know exactly where the circle is headed, according to the very premise of critical pedagogy. Circles are "space[s] in which all views can be voiced freely and safely. Only when all views are heard can we claim that the heterogeneous nature of our culture is most widely represented in the circle" (Steiner, Krank, McLaren, & Bahruth, 2000, p. 123).

Culture circles are grounded in problem posing, critical dialogue and problem solving. The aim is conscientization, or critical meta-awareness, of each participant's condition. The importance of the central components that ground this program was conveyed by Darder (2002),

> It is virtually impossible to speak of a revolutionary practice of problem-posing education outside the dialogical process, since dialogue is truly the cornerstone of the pedagogy. Central to Freire's concept of education is an understanding of dialogue as the pedagogical practice of critical reflection and action...This process of problem-posing serves to [promote]...the emergence of critical consciousness in the learning process... (p. 102)

But there were challenges too. As early as 1980, Bee reported that "Freire and his team needed to convince the people of their own worth,...[and] that no matter how denuded of dignity...they were in fact makers of culture, of history, and subjects in life, not merely objects of manipulation" (p. 40). To facilitate this process, Freire codified the generative themes into pictures, which he projected using what at the time were "state-of-the-art" slide projectors, thereby allowing the students to discuss situations relevant to them without exposing themselves individually or making themselves vulnerable. The pictures captured the generative themes lived or expressed by students. They allowed students to start engaging in critical dialogue and problem solving, as the pictures posed problems that were part of their very own collective realities and cultural legacies. Dialogically, participants posed problems and decoded the pictures, which represented generative themes.

Generative Themes

In culture circles, prior to planning engagements and teaching, educators learn from the communities and cultural practices which participants navigate. According to Freire (2000):

> The concept of a generative theme is neither an arbitrary invention nor a working hypothesis to be proved. If it were a hypothesis to be proved, the initial investigation would seek not to ascertain the nature of the theme, but rather the very existence or non-existence of themes themselves. In that event, before attempting to understand the theme in its richness, its significance, its plurality, its transformations, and its historical composition, we would first have to verify whether or not it is an objective fact; only then could we proceed to apprehend it. Although an attitude of critical doubt is legitimate, it does appear possible to verify the reality of the generative theme—not only through one's own existential experience, but also through critical reflection on the human-world relationship and on the relationships between people implicit in the former. (p. 97)

In culture circles, initially generative themes are codified into generative words which are broken down into syllabic parts and used to build or generate new words. Alternatively, the sociocultural and historical foundations of issues experienced by participants are problematized and deconstructed. These generative themes are codifications of complex experiences in the lives of the participants. They have political significance and are likely to generate considerable dialogue geared towards action.

Codification is the representation of a meaningful aspect of the learners' relevant life experiences and may possibly include a photograph or a drawing, a single word or an entire story. According to Paulo Freire (2000):

> It is to the reality which mediates men, and to the perception of that reality held by educators and people, that we must go to find the program content of education. The investigation of what I have termed the people's "thematic universe"—inaugurates the dialogue of education as the practice of freedom. The methodology of that investigation must likewise be dialogical, affording the

opportunity both to discover generative themes and to stimulate people's awareness in regard to these themes. Consistent with the liberating purpose of dialogical education, the object of investigation is not persons (as if they were anatomical fragments), but rather the thought-language with which men and women refer to reality, the levels at which they perceive that reality, and their view of the world, in which their generative themes are found. (p. 96)

The benefit of this representation is that it allows the students to analyze the situation from a non-threatening theoretical viewpoint while still making connections with the situation of their own lives (Heaney, 1989). There are no textbooks adopted in these circles, but culture notebooks instead—books created by the students themselves. Culture notebooks are made by the students and may include photos, drawings, word lists, and eventually stories generated and discussed in the culture circles.

"Through debate and detailed analysis of linguistic features, the members of the popular culture circle begin to discuss culture as a result of the human labor and the creative acquisition of human experience" (Freire, 2000, p. 69). Consequently, participants are able to engage in deeper dialogue, as the method focuses on their strengths, on their knowledge regarding those words and themes that emerged from their own universe, as opposed to accentuating the areas in which their practices might need further honing. This is done as participants "come to understand that reading and writing are not neutral acts; rather, they are linked to cultural practices that make political, epistemic, and moral claims on our lives" (Freire, 2000, p. 69).

Problem Posing

During this phase, participants pose problems as they try to understand a situation. Participants question practices that are taken for granted within their own contexts, allowing them to become critically aware of the origin and meaning of the values they've grown accustomed to calling their own. In doing so, they ask questions such as: "Why do you think this is happening?" "Who could help you with this?" "But...how did it get started?" "How does it affect class-room/family/work dynamics?"

As participants problematize the situation presented (codified representations of a common phenomenon which occurs in partici-pants' lives), they start dialoguing and listening to each other. According to the teachers who participated in in-service culture circles (Chapter 6), this happened because "they can relate to what's going on." Freire (1997) used this problematization or the technique of problem posing to initiate dialogue. Through dialogue (the next stage), we open the doors of possibility to rethinking our practices. According to Freire (1997):

> The task of the dialogical teacher in an interdisciplinary team working on the thematic universe revealed by their investigation is to "re-present" that universe to the people from whom she or he first received it - and "re-present" it not as a lecture, but as a problem. (p. 90)

Hence, problem posing or problematization that is relative to each learner's experience is key to transformative, liberatory education.

Through sharing oppressive issues plaguing their lives, participants problematize socially constructed definitions and values that had previously been conceived as absolute truths. Becoming critically meta-aware of how the social structure influenced their realities, participants are gradually able to deconstruct these definitions and locations in society and engage in re-working and re-envisioning their place in society in agentive ways. The role of the problem-posing educator is to create, together with the students, a process in which they collectively engage in constant questioning and unveiling of realities within their own lives and experiences (Freire, 2000). Through problem posing, the roles of teacher and learner become blurred, as learners are teachers and teachers are learners.

Dialogue: More Than Concurrent Monologue!

According to Freire:

> In order to understand the meaning of dialogical practice, we have to put aside the simplistic understanding of dialogue as a mere technique. Dialogue does not

represent a somewhat false path...to elaborate on and realize in the sense of involving the ingenuity of the other. On the contrary, dialogue characterizes an epistemological relationship. Thus, in this sense, dialogue is a way of knowing and should never be viewed as a mere tactic to involve students in a particular task. (Freire & Macedo, 1995, p. 379)

Dialogue is more than side-by-side monologue in which two or more individuals seek to stand their ground. It is a learning process and it considers multiple perspectives as fundamental. JoBeth Allen (2007) reminded us that genuine dialogue is different from exchanges in which we debate and try to win. Dialogue differs from a conversation. Allen wrote that in genuine dialogue we come to understand others' perspectives and do not seek to indoctrinate others with our own perceptions and biases. She wrote that "dialogue is the encounter between people, mediated by the world in which they live...in order to name the world" (p. 68).

Dialogue is an inherent component of the critical cycle, which is at the heart of culture circles. In culture circles, dialogue allows teachers/facilitators to collectively construct knowledge about teaching that is theoretically sound and directly relevant to the realities of each and every participant. This represents a positive change from the more monologic (one-sided) nature of the traditional banking concept of education. In dialogue, teachers-learners start reconceptualizing their knowledge as they learn from each other and are inspired and challenged by others' practices, experiences, perspectives, and realities. "[A]s learners dialogue and transact with a wide range of texts and come to make meaning for themselves, that newly constructed meaning enters into dialogue with the mainstream and other cultures" (Fecho, 2004, p. 47).

Instead of listening to someone and then independently making the connection to their own practices and lives, dialogue allows participants to collectively imagine how to take agentive roles and transform their own realities. After all, "Learning to *read* the word...emerged from purposeful discussion of generative words and codifications through the medium of the spoken word. Dialogue provides the bridge between oral and literate forms of interpreting, understanding, and transforming the world" (Roberts, 2000, p. 91). Through dialogue, participants critically analyze their positions in and across communities of practice. In doing so, they engage in re-thinking their realities and practices.

Problem Solving: What Can Be Done?

Through dialoguing and sharing their stories, participants problem-solve. "Storytelling is a site for problem solving. Every day, many problem solving narratives happen and delineate roles, relationships, values, and worldviews" (Ochs, Smith, & Taylor, 1996, p. 95). Problem solving emerges from dialogue, and is geared toward action. After talking about the problem posed, participants collectively plot plans for action, which can take place at the personal and/or societal level. This process is illustrated across contexts in Chapters 3 to 7.

Dialogue can lead to problem solving and is intended to break the monological definition of situations and conditions lived by culture circle participants, challenging the deterministic vein in their lives. Dialogue is intended to bring multiple perspectives to an issue, to empower participants, and to break down the monological parameters of what they should be and how they should live their lives. It is a complex process, yet a powerful one.

Through dialogical problem solving, it is essential that participants make associations between their identities on multiple levels (Ladson-Billings, 1994) and view knowledge as socially constructed, as constantly re-envisioned, recycled, and shared by both teachers and students. The kind of thinking employed in dialogue "shifts the locus of authority from that of community and tradition to the individual who unifies thought and action in a new praxis" (Bowers, 1987, p. 129), moving towards dialogic problem solving.

Action: Towards Praxis

After naming the issues they experience day in and day out, partici-pants problematize the sociocultural and historical construction of

[handwritten marginal note: The church needs this! Imagine the good we'd do]

their so-called realities. Dialogically considering multiple perspectives while engaging in collective problem solving, participants begin carrying out their plans for action. These planned actions take place in both individual and societal realms.

In culture circles, participants engage in problematizing and collectively analyzing narratives, the everyday stories people tell. Collectively, they engage in deconstructing the multiple discourses shaping these narratives, challenging real-world issues and developing critical meta-awareness (Freire, 1970). Through this process, participants engage in uncovering and demystifying the social construction of their realities. This process of identifying and deconstructing institutional discourses within personal narratives (Souto-Manning, 2007) makes social interaction a space for norms to be challenged and changed.

Culture circles embrace the concept of praxis, which Freire (1970) described as "reflection and action upon the world in order to transform it" (p. 36). Culture circle participants engage in praxis by dialogically reflecting on the sociocultural and historical construction of its participants' realities. Beyond incorporating a focus on narrative in investigative and communicative practices, culture circles have immediate lifeworld (Habermas, 1987) implications. A culture circle is built within the lifeworld of its participants and based on an understanding of their unique agency—both individual and collective. This is consistent with an empowering agenda centered in theory and research that is tied to praxis—an engaged praxis that accounts for the deliberative capacity of all individuals. Thus, culture circles bring praxis to life by creating a process in which individuals engage simultaneously with the word and the world.

Freire (1970) proposed that as people engage in social action aimed to solve problems and address issues they identify in their own narratives, they become not only aware of the issues influencing their situations, but critically meta-aware of larger discourses and influences shaping these issues. Within the context of culture circles, this critical meta-awareness allowed participants to develop a relationship of appropriation (as opposed to colonization) with language (Chouliaraki & Fairclough, 1999), identifying, problematizing, taking a stand, and engaging in social action to change their situations while challenging the deterministic claim that "[w]e are stuck in the vicious circles of mutually reinforcing cultural and economic subordination" (Fraser, 1997, p. 33).

This approach emphasizes that the critical cycle present in culture circles is not the transmission or mastery of some specific body of knowledge, but is about people who learn to read and write words, to make sense of their own worlds, instead of living in a world that someone else is making sense of on their behalf. As evident in other studies (Souto-Manning, 2007; 2009), participation in these circles is also internalized, and allows participants to engage in critical meta-awareness, to become individually "conscientized." As they approach a situation, they consider multiple perspectives and problematize the issues in a critically conscious manner.

The collective nature of the culture circles allows participants to find the strength needed for self-empowerment as well as to "attain actualised, unique personhood (and) personal responsibility" (Lee, 1994, p. 24). Again and again, in the culture circles in which I was involved, participants conveyed that the problem-solving component of culture circles led to an increased confidence in their own abilities to embody agentive stances, feel better about themselves, project more hope into the future, and to become more empowered. Across contexts, I saw the process of problem solving leading to both personal and social change.

As exemplified in Chapter 4, through participation in a culture circle community, women and men who had been alienated from their cultural legacies were encouraged to recognize, scrutinize, and take action regarding their location in society and their oppression (Gutierrez and Lewis, 1998). This happened through the steady and recurring action-reflection-action chain of group behaviors, praxis (Freire, 1970), which involved dialogue and action (Freire, 1995). Praxis encompassed the action of participants in recognizing issues, describing or labeling them, and exploring ordinary, possible solutions.

Not only in the instances presented in Part II of this book, but in many others as well, culture circle facilitators helped groups recognize their potential and power to act upon and transform situations. According to Marsiglia (2003):

> The group becomes a laboratory for democracy where all opinions count...In becoming a transformative force, the group initially decides on small action steps, develops plans, and implements them. Once the course of action is implemented, the group reflects on its accomplishments and shortcomings, relates the outcome to the larger societal phenomena they are concerned about, and starts planning the next action step. Group members are more capable of challenging and rejecting messages from the larger society that says that nothing can be changed. (p. 84)

As participants carry out actions, they engage in a collective reflection process as they report back to the group and discuss what worked and what didn't. The group repeats the same process (problematizing, dialoguing, problem solving, and planning a course of action) if there are remaining issues that need to be addressed — and often there are! If all works well, they celebrate with other participants and engage in dialogue regarding the applicability of such actions across settings. If not, they continue to problematize issues collectively, seeking to find solutions which may lead to transformative actions.

By engaging in this process, taking vulnerable positions (Behar, 1996), a stronger community of learners is formed. They feel confident about their abilities to promote change in their own lives. Participants start conveying agency in their narratives as they engage in personal change. The hope is that by rewriting their stories and engaging in action and change on the personal level, participants will collectively promote social change.

In culture circles across time and space, participants link personal problems and political issues (Gutierrez and Lewis, 1998). Through the use of the critical cycle, Freire proposed that people themselves actively engage in listening to and considering other understandings, other perspectives, respecting diversity, questioning the status quo in hopes of change; in hopes of forming a more just society. As a group, participants start to envision their capacity for change, projecting future endeavors and seeking to promote social justice (Marsiglia and Zorita, 1996).

Learnings

Overall, culture circles tackle difficult, personal, societal, and genuine issues in a very authentic way. While culture circles do not promote immediate change on the societal level or intentionally disturb institutional power imbalances, they do expose alternative perspectives and understandings of issues, allowing participants to start developing tools to engage in critical meta-awareness at their own personal level to challenge the status quo. Change on the institutional level takes time and must start from those involved. If Freire had proposed a program to end all kinds of injustice, imposing his own solutions, he would have only added one more layer of institutional oppression, imposing his proposed solutions on the lives of others.

In implementing this culture circle approach, I learned that young children and adult learners find this pedagogical approach engaging and relevant. As I employed this kind of pedagogy across time and space, participants (especially pre-service and in-service teachers) expressed transformative, powerful comments such as "I can't wait to try this in my classroom" and "This is so helpful." In this book, I share this approach (and multiple situated representations of it) with you in hopes that it will inspire you to engage in reflective practice in your school and/or classroom. After all, such a pedagogical practice extrapolates the traditional realm of classrooms and schools as it considers:

> Education as the practice of freedom—as opposed to education as the practice of domination—denies that man [sic] is abstract, isolated, independent, and unattached to the world; it also denies that the world exists as a reality apart from the people. Authentic reflection considers neither abstract man [sic] nor the world without people, but people in their relations with the world. In these relations consciousness and world are simultaneous: consciousness neither precedes the world not follows it. (Freire, 2000, p. 81)

Looking Ahead

Chapters 3 through 7 present situated representations of culture circles. Each of these chapters portrays the use of the critical cycle with children and adults, pre-service and in-service teachers, in Brazil and in the United States. As you read the following chapters, I suggest that you try to focus on some of the common elements of such pedagogy as well as some of the differences across contexts. As Freire (1998) advocated, feel free to envision ways to recreate this pedagogy to promote the practice of freedom; after all:

> There is no such thing as a neutral educational process. Education either functions as an instrument that is used to facilitate the integration of the younger generation into the logic of the present system and bring about conformity to it, or it becomes "the practice of freedom." (Shaull, 2000, p. 34).

I sincerely hope that you will feel compelled to envision ways to facilitate the process whereby individuals think critically about their realities and seek to transform their worlds.

Part II:

Culture Circles
Across Contexts

CHAPTER 3

Culture Circles in an American First-Grade Classroom

> I aim to support reflection on how we as educators might transform our teaching practices so that we may better build on, and respond to, the diverse resources of our children.
>
> Dyson (2008, p. 14)

I n this chapter[1], I present a description of the learning and social action that unfolded through Freirean culture circles in my first-grade public school classroom. Through the analysis of representative literacy events, I highlight how first-grade students problematized the racially and socioeconomically segregated nature of pull-out educational programs in American schools, a clear and complex institutional issue that affected society, schooling, and students' lives. As you read this chapter, I invite you to focus on the role of culture cir-

---

[1] An earlier version of this chapter was published in: Souto-Manning, M. (2009). Negotiating culturally responsive pedagogy through multicultural children's literature: Towards critical democratic literacy practices in a first grade classroom. *Journal of Early Childhood Literacy*, 9(1), 53-77.

cles in problematizing the pressures and practices imposed by an age of educational accountability within the context of public education in the United States (Genishi & Dyson, 2009). I encourage you to pay particular attention to the role of the children and the teacher in setting up a favorable classroom environment in which transformative actions are not only allowed but dialectically encouraged. By allowing you to peek through my first-grade classroom window, I hope to highlight the possibilities of employing Freirean culture circles in primary grades for the benefit of challenging the status quo, promoting transformation, and ultimately, better serving the educational needs of all children.

Generative Theme

Taylor:	But that's not fair!
Kary:	Fair? That's dead wrong!
Tyron:	We have to do something about it.
Madison:	Does everybody know?
Teacher:	What?
Madison:	That we have segregation?
Ralph:	We know, but what can we do?
Derrick:	I think we have to share what we know. I don't think it is right.

This dialogue took place in my first-grade classroom as students (all names are pseudonyms) realized how racially and socioeconomically segregated pull-out educational programs were. In early childhood, young children are deeply concerned with issues of fairness (Paley, 1986). Vivian Gussin Paley (1986; 2007) affirmed that the three Fs of childhood are fairness, friendship and fantasy. Through friendships, the children above (as represented by Ralph and Derrick's voices) are interested in promoting fairness.

According to Paulo Freire (1970), the first step towards change and transformation is to name the issue. Too often, we are so immersed in the intricacies of the contexts that shape our lives that we do not recognize the social construction of situations which oppress us. The generative themes (touchstones of culture circles) serve this purpose—to identify the issues. Above, the children identified segregation as the issue. The situated representation of the phenomenon (Dyson & Genishi, 2005) was present in the form of pull-out programs.

As the children problematized the purpose of pull-out programs, they realized that even though the intentions behind such programs were good, in reality, they were not individualizing instruction, but segregating students along race and class lines. The enrichment programs, such as gifted services, typically served rich, White children. However, the recovery or remediation programs included those who came from lower socioeconomic status (SES) families, and often culturally, linguistically, and racially diverse families (Lee, 2002; Lucas, 2001). They realized that the intent of a practice did not justify its results.

Within the United States, schools have served a sorting function in society (Mehan, 1996; Villegas, 2007). This complex institutional issue, schools serving as sorting mechanisms (Parsons, 1959; Turner, 1960) in the United States, oppresses and affects the fabric of society and schooling, and had done so in the very lives of this group of first graders. In many American public schools, while there is great diversity in the student body, there is also a range of access to specific opportunities and services. For example, the largest group of students represented in special education programs is that of African American males—a group which used to be in segregated schools decades ago but, in many cases, are now in segregated classrooms (Coutinho & Oswald, 2000). By naming such sorting procedures and the effects on their own lives, students were promoting social justice, which often starts at the cultural awareness level or with conscientization efforts (Freire, 1995; Marsiglia, 2003). They were not only aware of the issue, but they were disrupting the commonplace by problematizing a social issue and understanding existing knowledge and structures as sociocultural and historical products (Lewison, Seely Flint, & Van Sluys, 2002; Shor, 1987).

This did not occur without a deliberate starting point. It required attention to process and tools. The process I employed centered around interrogating multiple viewpoints, making differences visible (Harste, Breau, Leland, Lewison, Ociepka, & Vasquez, 2000), examining competing narratives and writing counternarratives to dominant discourses, such as the one identified by the children in the discursive episode above. The process inherent to Freirean culture circles involved identifying a generative theme, posing problems to uncover the sociocultural and historical structures curtailing individuals' agencies, and dialogically negotiating ways to transform the situations. The tools I employed were children's books, first selected through a continuously generative process (Vasquez, 2001), and later representing social issues (Lewison, Seely Flint, & Van Sluys, 2002). Here I describe how multicultural books might serve as conversation starters, as codifications of generative themes. However, as tools, they do not do it all by themselves. Dialoguing, problematizing, and uncovering social issues in texts are nevertheless important to further the conversation.

In this chapter, I share the ways in which culture circles facilitated critical processes in a first-grade classroom. In doing so, I present a description of the learning and social action that unfolded in critical literacy events during the 2001-2002 academic year. The process reflects the role early childhood teachers can embrace as they seek to promote critical education. It illustrates how multicultural children's literature can serve as a way to foster critical conversations with young children.

Problem Posing

After identifying a generative theme which emanated from their own lives and experiences, the children engaged in posing problems. The common childhood practice of asking why was encouraged, rather than being suppressed. Questions, in fact, had catapulted them into this inquiry. As we went on with our day, several times teachers came and took certain students away from the classroom to go to special classes. These classes were meant to individualize instruction for children who had been identified as having a special need (special education or gifted) or were "at-risk."

In fostering friendships in the classroom, children started issuing invitations to their friends to come along as they were pulled out of the classroom. When these invitations were met with resistance, they started questioning. Some of the questions they asked were: "Why can't Luis go with me to STAR (the gifted program)?" and "Why does Mrs. Carvalho take all the children who speak Spanish?" Critical conversations took place as the children disagreed with the exclusionary practices proposed by the program. As a teacher, I assumed the role of a facilitator, and sought to help create an environment in which the children felt comfortable asking questions and questioning the system in place. Had I decided not to create this place for problem posing and dialogue, these conversations would have remained in the periphery of the classroom.

To access the important conversations and themes in the classroom, I had left recording devices throughout the room. Following the conversation above (which took place in a whole group setting), I listened to some of the recordings made by these devices and encountered several conversations addressing the same topic. The excerpt below represents a peer conversation in which children code-switched to a more informal language. While temporally these conversations happened within a matter of days, contextual and linguistic differences are noticeable. I propose that this is due to the interactional context (Rymes, 2009) in which they took place.

William: We don't need no medicine. No fixin'! My momma be takin' good care o' me.
Johnnie: What you mean?
William: It's all 'bout tryin' to make ev'ryone same; but same's White; same's rich. I'm Black and I live in the project.

With that observation a six-year old boy, William, had captured the deficit perspectives often employed in American public schools; an extremely complex matrix of domination (Hill Collins, 1990). The generative theme (segregationist pull-out programs) was being problematized and social, historical, and cultural issues were being identified. The children were identifying situated representations of larger phenomena in their own classroom. Suddenly, issues of social justice became important and personal to these first-grade students. The structure in place was curtailing the children's agencies (Archer, 2003), but the children were questioning that structure. Creating critical spaces in the classroom and facilitating their dialogic exchanges helped them move from being discouraged by the lack of fairness, to holding hands with friends to fight injustices in order to change their worlds together (Vasquez, 2004).

In problematizing the issue, students engaged in sustained research, inquiring into the very reasons and history behind the supposed desegregation of schools (Gay, 2004). They came to uncover a very complex issue—Whites and Blacks were put in the same schools, but instead of a dialogue reconceptualizing educational practices, there were concurrent monologues in the form of pull-out programs (Freire, 1970). This problematization took place over several weeks in our classroom. We wanted to consider the complexities and complications of the issues. Students came to learn that when schools were integrated they were not really desegregated, as many continued to believe that the White culture was superior (Delpit, 1988; 1998), or at least maintained a stance that children from diverse backgrounds had to adapt to the dominant school culture. As an act of resistance, those in power created schools within schools, to continue serving the "brighter" children (read White, middle and upper SES) academically even if they had to be socially integrated with those believed to be inferior. The children realized that justice had not been served.

They found out that if a child's primary Discourse[2] (which Gee, 1996, defined as "big D" discourse and expanded beyond the traditional definition as language in use) was aligned with the school's primary discourse, that child experienced success and was seen as gifted. That is, those who knew how to talk the school talk and behave in ways that were desirable would likely do well; they were admired and privileged as they entered the school. However, if a child's language socialization processes differed from the one employed by teachers, they were diagnosed as needing help, as "at-risk" from day one (Delpit, 1998; Dyson, 1999).

At this point, the children were frustrated by the injustices they were experiencing. As a teacher, I knew that I needed to facilitate dialogue aimed at problem solving. I wanted to be careful not to impose my own views on my students. I wanted to enter this dialogue and learn from them and with them in an authentic way. As a teacher, I too had been frustrated by segregationist practices within schools. How could we do something together to change this in our context? How could we take matters of access and equity into our own hands? To address these questions, I engaged in critical teacher action research, a deliberate investigation, as students were engaged in the culture circle pedagogy.

Critical Theoretical Framework

As a teacher studying my own practice, I employed a critical theoretical framework. So did the students as they sought to negotiate change and transformation after documenting injustices. Together, in a very Freirean manner, we were reading our world (Freire & Macedo, 1987)

---

[2] Discourse is written elsewhere in the text with lowercase d for stylistic purposes. Nonetheless, discourse is defined as "...constructed not only by the language, but also by the objects, tools, technologies, sites and institutions (through which meaning is negotiated) that are put together in such a way that others *recognize* you as a particular type of who (identity), engaged in a particular type of what (activity) here and now" (Gee, 1996, p. 18).

in order to rewrite it in a more just way. We sought to challenge uneven power relationships (Anderson & Irvine, 1993).

Seeking to facilitate critical dialogue geared at problem solving and action in my own classroom, I employed Freire's (1990) concept of literacy as an introduction to democratization, conceptualizing learners as agentive subjects rather than recipients. I sought to challenge the banking concept of education in which knowledge is deposited into students' brains as money into a bank (Freire, 1970). In doing so, I sought to foster critical dialogue (rather than side-by-side monologue) which had the potential to transform and recreate relationships, fostering political and critical consciousness (Shor & Freire, 1987).

In a contextualized and situated manner, I employed Barbara Comber's (2003) application of critical literacy to working with young children, seeking to engage with local realities; mobilize students' knowledges, practices, and experiences; subvert taken for granted "school" texts; and collectively examine how power is exercised and by whom. These were the lenses that shaped this teacher action research study. After all, I realized that:

> Deconstruction without reconstruction or design reduces human agency; diversity without access ghettoizes students. Domination without difference and diversity loses the ruptures that produce contestation and change. (Janks, 2000, pp. 178-179)

Something had to be done. I knew it, but most importantly the children knew it. They had named the issue (generative theme) affecting their own lives and had not accepted it. They had uncovered and deconstructed (problematized) well-intentioned pull-out practices, and gone beyond face value. Dialogically, they had identified historical, cultural, and social issues shaping a larger phenomenon situated in our own first-grade classroom. Our diverse community of learners in my first-grade classroom realized that the lack of access to all programs and opportunities clearly ghettoized some students.

The Teacher

The role of the teacher, facilitator in a Freirean sense, in setting up a safe, comfortable environment in which children feel free to express their opinions is paramount. So often even in the early years, children enter classrooms and schools with a mindset that there are right and wrong answers to be assessed apart from contexts. Creating a community of learners, a sense of trust, and a respect for differences allowed us to engage in hard conversations. Nevertheless, we got started by using books, not to immediately personify the issues but as codifications of generative themes. Freire himself codified themes into pictures and drawings in culture circles in Brazil to get the dialogue started. Because of the availability, familiarity, and acceptance of books portraying social issues in early childhood settings, I decided to employ them as starting points as we sought to move towards authentic dialogue (Allen, 2007). The books were carefully selected in terms of their representation of issues identified within the context of the classroom or school. Thus, these books served as codifications of generative themes.

In the events described and analyzed in this chapter, my first-grade students and I read and discussed multiple texts about the civil rights movement, Martin Luther King, Jr., and Rosa Parks. These civil rights leaders were included in the state standards for first-grade, mandated after the *No Child Left Behind* federal legislation which sought to make educators and schools accountable for learning outcomes. Nevertheless, we went beyond the unit of study presented in our textbook and the typically happy endings portrayed in most children's literature to include media reports of discrimination in airports as more Blacks were stopped at security points, articles about unemployment rates, housing, and educational opportunities, and multiculturally oriented children's literature about civil rights and racism. By bringing multiple texts to serve as situated representations of our previously identified generative theme, I sought to provide the children with plenty of opportunities for problematizing the issue. As a result, they came to realize how prevalent issues of equity and access (or lack thereof) were in their immediate and not-so-immediate sur-roundings.

We went further than reading a paragraph about the civil rights movement and celebrating Martin Luther King Day. These first grad-ers explored multiple texts and versions of the civil rights movement and racism. This was of specific importance because the topic of civil rights and racism as traditionally presented in U.S. educational insti-tutions has been found to be problematic by many scholars working toward equitable educational environments (Ladson-Billings, 1994; Huber, Kune, Bakkem & Clark, 1997; Carger, 1996). Often due to White perspectives, African American children are silenced (Delpit, 1988) and not recognized for their knowledge, expertise, and experi-ences in American classrooms.

We dialogically problematized traditional and multicultural chil-dren's literature, as well as other texts (such as newspaper articles), considering multiple perspectives on the topic being discussed. In ex-ploring entryways to a classroom community that not only tolerated, but embraced diversities as resources, I wanted to foster the problem-atization of everyday issues and subsequent dialogue, considering a gamut of perspectives, experiences and definitions of knowledge. I wanted to live the concept of inclusion and value diversities.

Culture Circles in an Early Education Classroom

During the 2001-2002 school year I had a very diverse first-grade class. Students' out-of-school experiences were seemingly largely misaligned regarding tangible and intangible resources such as lin-guistic, cultural, social, racial and sexual backgrounds. I had 19 stu-dents. They lived in government-subsidized project homes, they lived in mansions owned by doctors, lawyers, and recording studio own-ers. They came from four-, three-, two-, and one-parent families. Some students had grandparents as primary caregivers and two students were in foster care. One child had two mothers. Another had an inter-racial family.

As these unique children brought background experiences and home literacies to the classroom, these experiences were not immediately recognized among the students as strengths. Such diverse cultural backgrounds initially clashed as they came together. Many students had been socialized into the knowledge as truth paradigm (e.g., "my way is the right way" and "this is how you do this"). Assumptions and beliefs that were exposed disrespected the very diversity present in our classroom. As a teacher seeking to foster equitable access to these unique students, I wanted to transform what seemed to be isolated individuals into a beautiful, collaborative learning community that valued each and every background represented in the classroom. Nevertheless, I knew that without reaching a place in which we respected diverse opinions and problematized our own assumptions, we would not survive the school year or form a collaborative learning community that provided access to diverse students. Unless we were able to recognize the realities of exclusion and isolation in our classroom (Janks, 2000), forming a community of learners that could build upon each others' strengths was a moot point.

After learning about ways to implement a collaborative learning community that would honor the diverse voices of children in the classroom, I deliberately and systematically employed participatory/ liberatory culture circle pedagogy. This framework of culture circles was originally employed in adult education (Freire, 1959) and had not (to my knowledge) been employed in an early childhood setting. Nevertheless, it was a generative framework that built upon participants' strengths. This participatory pedagogy allowed six- and seven-year-olds to engage in authentic dialogue (Shor & Freire, 1987), learning multiple perspectives as opposed to the right answer, the best way, or the absolute truth. I acted upon the belief that children's capacities were being underestimated in literacy classrooms (O'Brien, 2001a; Comber, 2003). In order to build on each others' strengths and grow as a learning community, children had to recognize the cultural nature of their own growth and development (Rogoff, 2003).

Freirean culture circles (an embodiment of this participatory/ liberatory pedagogy) were implemented throughout the year. Such a framework involved researching and learning about children's backgrounds and issues in the classroom. Together, we problematized those issues through problem posing, seeking to deconstruct the social construction of interactions and situations in the classroom in light of historical (and other) influences while engaging in dialogue. Through dialogue, collective problem solving took place, culminating in action. While presented quite linearly and briefly here, the process we employed was very recursive and cyclical (Souto-Manning, 2007) as further explained in Part I of this book.

Through representative snapshots, I present a temporal account of culture circles in my first-grade classroom. In doing so, I discuss how this framework was initiated (after students identified the issue organically), including common books telling classic stories, such as *The Three Little Pigs,* in the first month of school (early September, 2001). I write about how such a framework allowed my students and me to start problematizing local issues and recognize how they were shaped by larger, institutional structures, beliefs, and discourses. One example of how larger discourses shape local issues is the interplay between diversity and access, which can result in isolation, exclusion and the formation of ghettos (Janks, 2000).

As a result of listening closely to my students and engaging in dialogue with them, I explore the talk that took place in my first-grade classroom. Students learned to appropriate language—questioning language use and becoming aware of its power while considering alternative perspectives—(Chouliaraki & Fairclough, 1999) and started recognizing situated understandings. Recognizing the diversity in linguistic and cultural backgrounds as well as the validity of those differences allowed students to question educational experiences and the role of schools as sorting institutions, labeling some as "know-it-all" and others as "know-nothings." This concept of language appropriation, using language to question the status quo, rather than being colonized by it, aligns with Freire's work in which multiple perspectives are considered, many voices are heard, thereby helping "us to understand this obvious truth: No one knows it all; no one is ignorant of everything" (Freire, 1998, p. 39).

Considering Perspectives and Appropriating Language

Freire (1998) proposed in the quote above that humility is a core human value whereby individuals recognize that no one knows everything and no one is ignorant of everything. We all can learn and at the same time, we all have something to teach. As I sought to learn from my students, taking the stance of an ethnographer (Gregory, Long, & Volk, 2004) and blurring the roles of teacher and learner (Freire, 1970), I learned that the outlook to which most students had been socialized was a polarized model in which all things could be classified into right and wrong sides. This truth paradigm (Aronson, Harré, & Way, 1995) was hindering my efforts to foster a learning community allowing access to learners from diverse backgrounds—it was fostering exclusion and competition rather than inclusion and collaboration. To dispel this notion and engage in a systematic quest to promote change in my own classroom, I decided to use our read-aloud time to read books that told the same story from different perspectives. I wanted to promote the importance and validity of multiple voices in the classroom, and thought that starting with books authored in multiple voices would be a good beginning.

I chose to start with a classic story that most of them had heard, even in countries such as Mexico, Costa Rica, China, Korea, and Mongolia, and in the culturally, linguistically, racially, socioeconomically and sexually diverse backgrounds present in my class. I took a generative approach (Freire, 1970; Souto-Manning, 2007), in which I invoked families' knowledges and backgrounds, seeking to bring common experiences to the classroom. After asking parents about some of the classic stories read to children, I gathered that my students were all familiar with some version of "The Three Little Pigs." This is where I started.

First, I read Paul Galdone's *The Three Little Pigs* (1970). In this book, Galdone started with a traditional "Once upon a time..." and told the story of an old sow that did not have enough money to raise her three little pigs. Those pigs went off and met men who gave them straw, sticks, and bricks respectively. Once built, a wolf came along and blew down the houses made of straw and sticks and ate the pigs that inhabited them. However, the wolf was not able to blow down the house made of bricks. Eventually, he decided to climb through the last pig's brick chimney. The wolf slid down into a big open pot of boiling water, cooked, and was eaten as dinner by the little pig who "...lived happily ever afterward."

I then read James Marshall's *The Three Little Pigs* (1989), which uses more adjectives to describe the houses and rhythmic phrases such as "No, no, no, not by the hair of my chinny chin chin." Even though Marshall's version of the story was very similar to Galdone's, they were told and illustrated quite differently. As I read these two stories, students started theorizing from practice:

Kary: I get it...even when we read the same story, we can understand it differently!

Derrick: Yes! Did you see the pictures? They were so so so different.

Alexus: Yeah...but the story was the same.

Kasey: Almost, not really.

William: When you is readin' somethin', the pictures in your brain is different from pictures in my brain.

Kianna: But...which one is the right one?

Teacher: Right one?

Kianna: Yeah...

Teacher: What do you think? Is James Marshall right? Is Paul Galdone right?

((undecipherable talk))

Alexus: I think they are all right.

Teacher: Yes. Just because their stories are different, it doesn't mean that there is a right one and a wrong one.

William: That just mean they chose tal' different way, like sometime we was speakin' different in class.

Sanquitta: Like, the way we speak at home? [referring to African American English]

William: Yeah…ya know.

After reading these two books and talking about them, students started theorizing from their experiences. In the excerpt above, William said "When you is readin' somethin', the pictures in your brain is different from pictures in my brain." This reflects Rosenblatt's transactional theory (1978), in which each time a reader and a text transact, there is a unique poetry created, or as William put it, a different picture painted in your brain. Students related to their background experiences such as linguistic preferences according to context. For example, Sanquitta used African American English and the so-called Standard English as an analogy of the different pictures readers can paint as they read or wrote a story. Students were making sense of the concept of situated perspectives and how there were many ways to tell a story and to experience the world.

Following these two similar tellings of the same story, in which the authors framed the pigs as good and the wolf as bad, I shared Jon Scieszka's *The True Story of the 3 Little Pigs* with the class. In this story, the wolf told what really happened, explaining that he only wanted a cup of sugar to bake a birthday cake for his granny. The story starts by challenging previous assumptions, in which it reads "Everyone knows the story of the Three Little Pigs. Or at least they think they do. But I'll let you in on a little secret. Nobody knows the real story, because no one has ever heard my side of the story" (Scieszka, 1996). The wolf went on to tell that he didn't huff and puff as usual but rather had a very bad cold and sneezed, thereby blowing down the houses made of straw and sticks. As the houses fell down, and straw and sticks piled up, the pigs were "dead as doornails." The wolf said, "It seemed like a shame to leave a perfectly good ham dinner lying there in the straw. So I ate it up." The analogy of "a big cheeseburger just lying there" made many of my students empathize with the wolf.

The book uses some of the same language James Marshall did with a twist, such as "I am shaving the hairs on my chinny chin chin." In this story, the wolf was not boiled as dinner, but ended up in prison, and as headlines in newspapers.

William: I like this one the most.

Kasey: I think that we never got to hear the wolf's voice before.

Teacher: Yes, he offers us another perspective.

Luz: Pers-perspective?

Teacher: Yes. Another point of view; a different telling of the same story.

Alexus: So, it's not about right and wrong stories. It's about who writes it.

Shaniece: It's nice to know how the people, I mean the animals, see what happened.

Kary: This is very helpful.

Teacher: How so?

Kary: Now I think I get it. Now I get it. Just because someone does something in a different way, it doesn't mean that it is wrong. We should still listen to it, and understand, or at least try, how a person understands something. Like, in the books we read.

Derrick: Yeah...The pigs and the wolf told what happened in very different ways.

Taylor: And we can't even know what the two pigs who were eaten thought because they are dead.

The children started questioning their previous assumptions of right and wrong, understanding authorship and valuing, or at least respecting, different voices; multiple perspectives. By recognizing the importance and validity of multiple perspectives, students could understand the importance of authentic dialogue. They discussed purpose and different ways of knowing. From a comparison perspective in which knowledge and actions are judged against their own, students started seeing practices that differed from theirs as equally valid. This happened not only in this dialogue, but in many others throughout the year. Students engaged in dialogue constantly as they identified issues affecting their very lives and problematized them, seeking to move towards collective and dialectically negotiated transformative action. The students and I talked about the concept of voice and authorship (as mentioned above by Alexus) as well as the role of stereotype and previous knowledge and experiences in shaping expectations.

Although common works of children's literature, these books codified generative themes and served to set the tone for our classroom. Multiple perspectives (or authorings) became a valid concept in the classroom and children sought to learn from each other and how their peers experienced school. Such a framework allowed children to start naming some of the issues in school (such as its sorting function), making visible some of their experiences that granted access in a segregated manner.

Considering perspectives and appropriating language were pivotal and important aspects of the change that took place. This culture circle framework fostering open-ended dialogue that valued multiple voices became a common occurrence in the classroom, hence the importance of describing it here. While situated in the beginning of the school year that started in 2001, this is a representative episode which illustrates how dialogue enabled transformation when multiple perspectives were considered.

We continued to consider multiple perspectives, voices, and experiences in texts as well as in classroom activities. The children had been socialized into problem-posing education and questioned many of our classroom routines and structures. We continued to work at considering multiple voices and sought to foster a classroom environment that was inclusive of a multiplicity of voices and backgrounds.

Dialogue, Problem Solving, and Action: Challenging Racism Today

About four months later in January, 2002, multiple perspectives informed discussions of books, including the one below, exposing social issues such as racism:

Kasey: I liked the book [The Story of Martin Luther King Jr.]!
Shaniece: Me too!
Teacher: Tell me something that you were not sure about.
Johnnie: Uh…the schools.
Taylor: Yeah.
Annie: Why Blacks chose to go to old schools?
Jorge: They might like it better.
William: No way! I don't think so!
Diego: And the Whites liked newer schools better.
Sanquitta: They had more money; that's why they got to go to the newer school; to the better school.
Luz: So, there were only White people in one school and only Black people in the other?

This conversation took place after reading *The Story of Martin Luther King Jr.,* by Johnny Ray Moore (2001). I was amazed to hear such a conversation. Despite the fact that we had been problematizing social constructions and structures for four months on a daily basis, children were not able to apply such a framework, such a stance, to a wider context. In the excerpt above, Diego and Jorge stated their perceptions that African Americans were in older schools and Whites were in newer schools because of their preferences. This clarified the need to explore historical underpinnings of racism and segregation.

While I had regarded books as catapults for the problematization of everyday issues such as prejudices, reading this book had not gotten us there. This was coherent with Jennifer O'Brien's study on how children's books limit inquiry (2001b). The excerpt above illustrates how a book can be misunderstood, and how it serves only as a tool for critical dialogue and action. The talk that goes on around the book is as important as, if not more important than, reading the book itself. It is the role of the teacher to facilitate the dialogue and to pay special attention to the critical turns, supporting them, so as to scaffold problem solving and action (Freire, 1970). I must add a note of caution here: there are many American picture books that impart the sociohistorical influences of segregation more openly. While this book explored segregation, it did not explore the untold stories and historical influences of the phenomenon.

It became necessary to read books that more openly explored the issues of segregation and how they applied to the lives of children. I selected realistic fiction books. As we read a variety of multicultural books such as *Goin' Someplace Special* (McKissack, 2001), *The Other Side* (Woodson, 2001), *Freedom Summer* (Wiles, 2001), *White Socks Only* (Coleman, 1996), and *The Story of Ruby Bridges* (Coles, 1995), students started problematizing the social issues portrayed by these books. I sought to provide a variety of perspectives, including stories of girls and boys in times of segregation, stories of inclusion and exclusion. This led students to problematize school-wide gender discrimination as discussions and teachings centered around Martin Luther King, Jr., not dismissing the importance of Dr. King in the civil rights movement, but problematizing blatant exclusion from other perspectives. As students read these books, they developed empathy for the characters, delved into larger social issues and expanded the sphere of their problem posing beyond our classroom walls.

For example, as we read *Goin' Someplace Special* and *The Story of Ruby Bridges*, the children started realizing how the issues affected them. Many of them empathized with the stories that took place in the 1950s and 1960s in the United States. Yet, the issues the books raised guided students to think of their own locations of oppression within the school and society. They started sharing their own stories, generating themes for discussion. In *Goin' Someplace Special*, Tricia Ann experiences racism and segregation in Nashville (a Southern city, similar to theirs). This story portrays the first time Tricia Ann is allowed to go outside her community all by herself. Knowing the dangers and prejudices she is likely to experience, Tricia Ann's grandmother prepares her well, invigorating her "with enough love, respect, and pride to overcome any situation." As Tricia Ann makes her way to visit the public library, where she is allowed in, she grows frustrated by the Jim Crow laws that prohibit her, an African American, from entering a number of restaurants and hotels and from sitting on park benches marked "For Whites Only." She's evicted from a hotel lobby and insulted as she walks by a movie theater, "Colored people can't come in the front door," she hears a girl exclaiming to her brother. She almost gives up, but remembers the words of loved ones. "Carry yo'self proud," one of her grandmother's friends tells her. Tricia Ann at last arrives at a special place, a place Mama Frances calls "a doorway to freedom"—the public library.

Many of the children in my first-grade classroom did not realize that going to the library was something special and that special benches and entrances existed at one time for Blacks and Whites. Going to the library and being able to sit on the same bench (or any bench they wished) was, for them, something taken for granted. But were they really able to sit wherever they wanted and to enter through whichever door they wished? As we discussed Tricia Ann's situation and restrictions, the children started drawing parallels between larger segregation and sorting in their school context. Comments such as, "is it like when we want to go to STAR but can't?" referring to the school's gifted program. They were problematizing and naming (Freire, 1970) some of the school's sorting structures (Mehan, 1996).

As we continued reading, the children continued to draw parallels and become involved with the structure that curtailed their agency within the sphere of schooling. *The Story of Ruby Bridges* (Coles, 1995), the first African American girl to attend a New Orleans elementary school after court-ordered desegregation in 1960, describes how a six-year-old walks past angry crowds of White protestors to enter the school only White children traditionally attend. Yet, when she gets in, she is all alone. Parents of the White students kept them home. Ruby "began learning how to read and write in an empty classroom, an empty building." In a somewhat romanticized ending, the story progresses until two boys and then the rest of the students return to school; the mobs disperse by the time Ruby enters second grade. My students engaged in dialogue such as the one below:

William: I get it. It's just like us.

Teacher: Like you?

William: Yeah. It's like when you don't know you goin' special ed, to resource, and you thin' you special. Then you know later that you really dumb. You all alone, ya' know. We all here in yo' class, but when we go to tha' other class, it's not everybody.

Derrick: And how everyone who goes to STAR [pseudonym for the county's gifted education program] is White.

Kary: Wow...

Shaniece: I don't know...

Luz: But we go to the same school.

Derrick: Just think...

Johnnie: Yeah, Derrick. I'm not really sure.

Erin: Well, there's a way. Let's find out. ((Erin goes to the easel and grabs the marker. She writes the names of the teachers who teach in pull-out programs))

Teacher: What are you going to do?

Erin: I am going to find out how many go with each teacher

Teacher: How will this help you get to what you want to know?

William: Yeah. How?

Derrick: We can choose different color markers for boys and girls, and then...

Madison: No, no, I know. If we are talking about Black and White, we need to get black and white markers.

Ci'Erikka: White marker?

Madison: Well, like we read, we are not really white. So, let's choose pink.

((Erin grabs a pink and a black marker))

Jorge: Here is the brown.

Erin: Oh yes, I forgot.

Kary: We can't forget anyone.

Even though my students were not aware of many of the complexities of the matrix of domination described by Hill Collins (1990) and the way gender, class, and race served as sorting devices in schools and in society (Parsons, 1959; Turner, 1960) they charted themselves and discovered that all children who received gifted services were from White or Asian backgrounds. All the children who received ESOL (English to Speakers of Other Languages) services were Asian or Latinos. All those going to resource (receiving Special Education services) were African American children, actually African American boys. They had problematized and uncovered racial and gender segregation, covert racism, and sexism in our own school.

My students were not quite sure why that happened or if the inequity just happened by accident—the fact that all receiving interrelated special education services were Black males, for example. After much talk, they decided that they could not really find out if the segregationist practice so intrinsic to American public schools (Andrews et al., 2000; Delpit, 1988; 1998) today was accidental or if there was a systemic issue. Nevertheless, they seemed to draw connections to the stories they had read and invoked the socio-historical context of segregation and racism often in their conversations. Without getting bogged down by how that happened, but acting upon the need to change the situation, they engaged in authentic dialogue and decided that we had to do something about it—problem solve and take action. They also noticed that the teacher offering gifted services was called *Dr.* while the others were *Mrs.* What did that mean? That she had received more preparation? Why were only the smarter kids getting the "teacher that knew the most?," as one of them put forth. These were very deep and important questions that I had considered more than once as a teacher who wanted the best for her students.

These six- and seven-year-olds were becoming aware of segregation by ability associated with skin color. Nevertheless, they decided that something needed to be done about it and that every child could use a bit of extra support. They decided to call our principal in and talk to her, sharing what they had learned. Our principal agreed that something had to be done—but what? She suggested we keep talking, acknowledging the importance of the issue the first graders voiced and asked that when we found a solution or had some more information, to please share it with her. While the children were happy with her response and felt that they could change things, I thought that she was just trying to put us off and felt very discouraged as indicated by my journal entries.

Despite my discouragement, the children's resolve was contagious. I could not let them down after seeking to provide access to the best educational experience each and every one of them could have. We continued our quest and tried to find a solution together. After problematizing their locations and narratives, using multicultural literature as starting points, the children started valuing their very own locations and experiences. What did it feel like to go to STAR? To ESOL? To resource (special education)? What did it feel like to work with the reading teacher (Reading Recovery)? What did they do in each of these classes? These were some of the questions asked. They uncovered the very dissonant feelings and realities associated with going to each class—from a structured phonics resource program to an inquiry-based curriculum (Hill, Stremmel, & Fu, 2004) in the STAR classroom. These were sincere conversations in which the children vulnerably shared their experiences. According to the students, they shared their experiences (positive and negative) because they trusted each other and now felt part of a community. They also thought that unless they had the information from many people, listening to many voices, they could not have a clear picture of the situation.

Finally, after much dialogue in which we co-constructed knowledge, students decided that they all would like to engage in inquiry studies as described by those students receiving gifted services. They suggested that instead of being segregated in these pull-out programs, the just thing to do would be to give every student access to these different teachers and programs, problem solving and planning a course for action that would affect their own lives.

By becoming aware of the issue, these six- and seven-year-olds came up with a very appropriate and plausible solution. Change did not come quickly. While the principal initially was available to talk with us, she was reluctant to make the suggested changes. Change started with the children yet again. During Spring conferences, children presented their portrait of a learner to their parents and one by one expressed the desire to be together with this group of friends and learners one more year. They also petitioned their parents that they wanted to be in the same classroom all the time, throughout the school day. It was easier to gain the support from the parents of children who were receiving special education services and early intervention. The harder work was to convince the parents of the students receiving gifted education that they wanted to stay in the classroom. Six- and seven-year-olds took the lead and I offered to explain how this could be a good experience for all learners.

Upon gathering the support from 17 of the 19 parents, I went on to talk with the principal. I asked her if I could teach this amazing group of students in second grade and if she would allow me to serve these students in the classroom without pull-out classes. She seemed reluctant at first, but upon hearing of the parental support I had gathered, she agreed to consider. "But you will have to talk with the other teachers and work with their schedules. It will be a lot of extra work for you," she said. I met with the resource, the early intervention, and the ESOL teacher. They all agreed to adopt a push-in model for my class. They were each in my second-grade classroom for 40-50 minutes a day serving as another teacher. Having taught mostly the same students the previous year, I started co-teaching with the ESOL, STAR, and resource teachers. They no longer taught certain children, but all children in the classroom. Therefore, the following pieces had to be in place for this to happen: (1) student support; (2) parental support; (3) administrative support; (4) collegial support; (5) my resolve to invest whatever time and efforts it took to make this work (including teaching the same group of children again, expending additional time for planning and teaching under pressure for a while). Of course this is not an exhaustive list, but only a basic list of what had to happen for this change to occur.

The main obstacle was to convince the STAR teacher (who served gifted students) that all children could learn in an inquiry-based curriculum. She was skeptical at first, and so were some of the parents. As the school year started, some of the parents of students eligible for STAR classes were still reluctant and took this experience as a trial. One of the parents said that her daughter could try for nine weeks (one grading period) and then she would decide whether the daughter would remain in my second grade or move to another classroom.

The major difficulties I experienced were 1) proving to parents this would benefit all children and not just serve as a gift to those receiving remedial classes/services, and 2) coordinating my classroom time with the other teachers. There was a lot of pressure as parents of gifted students chose to visit my classroom with a judging demeanor to check and see what their children were doing. I am happy to report that these skeptical parents turned into supportive adults in the classroom after seeing how much their children were learning. Also, as I co-planned with three teachers, I had to coordinate my schedule with theirs and some days did not leave school until 6:00pm even though our school day was over at 2:30pm. Collaborating teachers were gracious about their time, but I worry about what would have happened if all teachers were adopting such a model and how planning would be even more challenging. I am not stating this to illustrate how impossible this would have been, but to say that this is an area needing to be addressed. It would be idealistic and romantic to say that there were no difficulties—there were! Nevertheless, I believe that the benefits far outweighed the challenges. Now, having only applied such a model to one group of children, I am not fully aware of the obstacles to implementing such a model on a wider scale. Whatever the difficulties, I am confident the children's voices would support this model for all. For example, the excerpt that initiates this article represents a subsection of this larger discussion. By suggesting that the school structure should be changed, they were writing their counter-narratives (Lewison, Seely Flint, and Van Sluys, 2002) based not only on writing words, but re-writing their classroom worlds (Freire, 1970) as they engaged in Freirean culture circles.

CHAPTER 4

Culture Circles in a Brazilian Adult Education Program

...no educational experience takes place in a vacuum, only in a real context—
historical, economic, political, and not necessarily identical to any other context.

Freire (1985, p. 12)

I n 1964, the year in which a president should have been elected in Brazil, the military took the government forcefully. Democracy came to a halt in Brazil and Paulo Freire's culture circles were outlawed. The coup d'etat came as Freire's culture circles were yielding rapid and remarkable results. Peasants were questioning their location in society and engaging in social action to improve their conditions. These culture circles were so successful that they were threatening the new military government, thus within 14 days of the coup d'etat, they were extinguished. Some 20 years later, they again became a reality as a democratic government was re-established in Brazil. This chapter[3] outlines the power and possibilities afforded by

---

[3] An earlier version of this chapter was published in: Souto-Manning, M. (2007). Education for democracy: The text and context of Freirean culture circles in Brazil. In D. Stevick and B. Levinson (Eds.), *Reimagining civic education: How diverse nations and cultures form democratic citizens*. Lanham, MD: Rowman-Littlefield.

Freirean culture circles within the historical and political context of contemporary Brazil and their role in education for democracy, as praxis for change.

Context and Historicity of Culture Circles in Brazil

Historically, illiteracy has been a reality for Brazilians. In 1890, 67.2% of Brazilians were illiterate (Haddad & Freitas, 1991). In 1920, even though a republic had been established, 60.1% of Brazilians were still illiterate. In Brazil, the first large adult literacy campaign occurred in 1947 (Yamasaki & Santos, 1999), after the end of the Vargas dictatorship. During the 1950s, there was no specific method to teach adult literacy. According to Yamasaki and Santos (1999), "the illiterate adult was made responsible for his/her condition, being considered incapable of taking on responsibilities; society was not given...any historical responsibility for this social exclusion" (p. 7). Psychologically, the illiterate adult was classified as having serious learning problems, and treated as a child. This contributed to the marginalization of these adults as well as to prejudice, limiting the social and political effectiveness of the illiterate adult in the world in which he/she lived (Ribeiro, 1997).

With emancipatory theories in the 1950s, these adults came to be recognized as "victims of an exclusionary historical-social process" (Yamasaki & Santos, 1999, p. 8). Haddad and Freitas (1991) blamed the still extremely high Brazilian illiteracy rate of 46.7% at the end of the 1950s on the lack of a specific pedagogical approach to teach adult literacy that involved the situated contexts of the learners and that engaged them in purposeful or meaningful learning.

As outlined in Part I of this book, during the 1950s, Freire developed a new vision for the pedagogical process of an adult literacy program that involved not only learning how to read the word, but how to read the world. Freire's method invited students to learn and value their own cultures and histories while questioning the system in place, contrary to the common misconception that his method consisted of a White middle-class man making decisions and imposing his judgments on the lives of others (Keesing-Styles, 2003).

Culture circle participants analyzed their own situations as they started to mobilize against the system in place, a system in which they had been subject to very poor living conditions and very few opportunities for change. They collectively started reading words and worlds as they sought to develop ways to write their futures based on critical readings of their pasts and the sociocultural forces that shaped their histories and locations. They wanted people like them in power; they wanted to be part of a true democracy (Instituto Paulo Freire, n.d.b).

From 1960 to 1963, Freire was involved with the Popular Culture Movement (Movimento de Cultural Popular, MCP) in Recife. Gerhardt (1993) reported that Freire's literacy method, the culture circles, were first implemented and developed in an MCP group which Freire coordinated in one of the suburbs of Recife. Paulo Freire was invited by the mayor of Recife at the time, Miguel Arraes, to construct and implement a larger literacy program under the umbrella of the MCP (Taylor, 1993). Taking a critical perspective, this program was to start the process of transformation through education (de Castro, 1969).

Having successfully implemented this powerful program in Recife, Freire was invited by the governor of Rio Grande do Norte, another Northeastern Brazilian state, to head a pilot project in the city of Angicos. Angicos happened to be the governor's hometown; he wanted to do something significant for his town, especially considering elections would occur in the following year, 1964. Freire agreed to work in Angicos, but made it clear to the governor that he was not going to campaign in the classroom to convince voters to vote for the incumbent. Freire then recruited the help of university students to conduct these culture circles and foster liberation through education.

In 1964, the circles were extinguished by the military government and Freire was exiled. While in exile, he continued developing his work in other Latin American countries, in North America, Europe and Africa. According to Senge et al. (2000):

> Freire['s]...success in the national adult literacy campaign in Brazil in the 1960s influenced literacy campaigns around the world...Freire believed that literacy was one means to democracy, and felt that being able to "read the word" was intimately tied to being able to "read the world"—that is, to analyze the political and social conditions that circumscribe people's lives, in order to envision how these conditions should be changed. (p. 208)

In the late 1980s, following a two-year transition from a military to a democratic government, culture circles were re-established in Pernambuco, becoming the national model for adult literacy programs (*Educação de Jovens e Adultos*). The culture circle I describe here was part of this program serving adults in the state of Pernambuco (Secretaria de Educação e Esportes, Governo do Estado de Pernambuco, 1997).

These circles were based on the belief that education is a social process, "a process of living and not a preparation for future living" (Dewey, 1897). Thus, the purpose of Freirean culture circles wasn't to aid people in accepting, complying, and functioning better within a given system. Instead, Freire wanted the oppressed to become aware of injustices and to act and change them (Finger & Asún, 2001).

A Culture Circle in Action

On a Monday evening in June, 2003, as darkness began to settle and the heat gave some signs of weakening, women and men, from late teens to early seventies, started entering the room in which they routinely met for their culture circle. Some of them came right from work, which could be noted by their clothes and hands dusted with soil, signaling their agricultural employment. Some of them talked about the work on the tomato farms in the region, as many of them were engaged in this kind of work. Others looked tired, as if ready to go to bed. It was almost seven o'clock. The facilitator was there, but could hardly be identified apart from the participants as she sat and talked with some of them. There wasn't an official start routine. Conversations about everyday themes and issues that started small developed to a point in which they involved all, as they engaged in dialogue and problem solving; two inherent parts of the culture circles.

From the beginning, work was clearly the topic of the night. Whether in the tomato fields or in someone's kitchen, they all kept hard work schedules; many led double journeys, double lives, working harshly inside and out of their homes. While the facilitator had positioned herself as an ethnographer of the community in the past, this culture circle had now grown into a trustful community of learners. While Sandra (the facilitator) kept in touch with the community, she no longer had to enact the role of documenting the most urgent, oppressive issues experienced by the circle participants. The stories they brought with them became generative themes to be (de)codified through problem posing by the collective. Participants told stories and conveyed their everyday narratives (Ochs & Capps, 2001) which in turn became sites for collective problem solving (Ochs, Smith, & Taylor, 1996).

As circle literants started talking about their work, money and salary emerged naturally as the conversation point, as a theme to which they could all relate. As many of them conveyed stories of everyday, recurring oppressions, they codified their generative themes as Sandra had done in the past. Josi expressed her frustration by saying:

> It doesn't matter how much I work, I am always owing something to someone; I am always late with my bills. I live with fear, fear that one day I will get home and not have enough money to pay the rent, or to give food to my children.

Participants, men and women. nodded. Another woman, Solange, asked Josi, "But don't you make a minimum [wage] salary?" Josi answered positively. "What does that mean?" asked Sandra, the facilitator. Solange immediately answered, "That means she should have enough to live." As they sought to establish the importance of the issue for the collective, they engaged in the following dialogue:

Josi: I work hard, but the salary is not enough. I don't know what I am doing wrong—

José: —Wrong?

Josi: Yes, because I work, earn a minimum [wage] salary, but it's never enough to pay the bills and put food on the table.

Solange: But the minimum [wage] salary is enough. Isn't it? ((looks around seeking approval))

Miriam: I don't have enough money for all my bills either. Do you have—

Solange: —What? Enough money?

Josefa: Yes—

Solange: —No. I am not the owner of my own house. I pay rent every month. I can't buy everything that my family needs. Some days all we eat is [manioc] flour. A handful of flour to fill the belly. We don't have meat on the table.

((Many nod, showing agreement and empathy))

The group started talking about the minimum wage salary and how most of them could identify with Josi's situation. They all made minimum wage salaries, which according to governmental definition, should allow for a decent living, but they arrived at the conclusion that it didn't, at least in their experiences. They worked hard, but the minimum wage established by federal law was what most of them earned. Some earned even less.

After arriving at the understanding that the minimum wage salary wasn't allowing most of them to lead a decent life—to have food on the table and to pay utility bills and housing expenses—they started problematizing the definition of a minimum wage salary.

José: So who decided how much is enough?

Marina: I don't know. It wasn't me.

((laughter))

Solange: Who was it?

((side talk as they try to figure out who sets the minimum wage salary))

Sandra: The government is who approves the minimum [wage] salary—

Josi   —That's not fair. They don't earn a minimum salary. I just saw Lula [the Brazilian president] in a big car on a store's television. I can't buy a car like that. I can't even pay to go to work by bus. I go walking.

Miriam: Me too.

Solange: Who earns a minimum [wage] salary?

((most raise their hands))

Solange: Who earns less than a minimum [wage] salary?

((four women raise their hands))

José: Do you work the entire day?

Laurinda: I work—

Neto: —the entire week?

((women who earn less than the minimum wage nod))

Laurinda: Who earns more than the minimum [wage] salary?

((five of the eight men in the room raise their hands))

Sandra: What do you perceive?

Luís: That we earn more than they [do].

Solange: Men earn more money—

Neto: —but it's not enough to live.

The women and men in the culture circle realized that there was economic injustice. The government had established the minimum wage as the lowest amount a person was to be paid to be able to live on, yet this amount was not enough. They went on to talk about the fact that those establishing the minimum wage amount did not make minimum wage salaries themselves, therefore they had no idea of what was "enough." Within literants' context, it was clear that the minimum wage was not adequate.

In addition to uncovering the social economic status issues regarding minimum wage—those who made higher wages established the minimum wage but did not have to live by it—circle participants also uncovered gender discrimination in terms of salaries. The gender issue erupted through the problematizing of salaries as a theme of discussion. This cyclical and recursive nature of the culture circle pedagogy allowed multiple layers of issues to be uncovered and problematized. The salary issue being discussed was definitely linked to economic and historical injustices, but was made more complex by the addition of gender to the mix. As Pat Hill Collins (1990) explained, the matrix of oppression considers the complexities of intersections of different dimensions of social inequality. Even though the minimum wage salary was clearly not enough to lead a decent life in the experience of this culture circle's participants, the women had a clear disadvantage as they made less money than the men. Women earned less money even when they worked at the same place and performed the same kind of job, as was the case with two circle participants, Neto and Miriam.

After much discussion, dialogue, and reflection on the issue of economic and gender-based discrimination and injustice, the participants decided to take action. Their course of action was to name the issue—the unlivable and inhumane nature of the Brazilian minimum wage. They wanted to raise the awareness of those who were making decisions, setting the minimum wage salary.

They started by calculating (instead of speculating) what would be a decent, livable, minimum wage. After adding housing, utility, and transportation to and from work, clothing, and food (not restricted to manioc flour and water) for a family of three, they arrived at 650 *reais* (Brazilian currency), which amounted to around three minimum wage salaries at the time, or approximately 230 U.S. dollars. They did not include any luxuries, and based their calculations on average amounts spent by participants in the group. They did not intend to ask politicians to set a salary that would allow them to change their socioeconomic statuses, just to be able to pay their current bills and lead an honest life.

They concluded that session by charting two plans of action—one at the personal and one at the societal level. On the personal level, they were going to further their studies so as to be better qualified to take on better-paying jobs. They knew that while education would not be the sole answer to changing their lives, it gave them tools to advance professionally. Both men and women also decided to ask their employers why the women were making less money than men for the same job.

Bridging the personal and the institutional realms, they were determined to attempt to dialogue with their employers about the importance of equal pay across genders for the same kind of work. This was a courageous action, as many of them were at the bottom of the hierarchy in terms of employment and could be putting their livelihoods and employments at stake. Nevertheless, they felt this was important and strategized ways to let their employers know that they were aware of the issue and did not agree with it. They asked for change, and many of them were able to compel their employers to action. They also understood that their employers' decisions were not made out of personal spite, but shaped by the more recent inclusion of women in the workforce and the perception that men were heads of households and therefore should make more money. Being able to see what their employers' rationales were raised many other issues of which the circle participants had not been previously aware.

On the larger institutional level, literants decided to write a letter to their representatives in state and national government that conveyed their experiences with the minimum wage salaries. They wrote not only of the difficulties they were experiencing as they could not make ends meet, but stated that "Three salaries is what allows [us] to live. [We] have to study very much..." The letter ended by calling for action on the institutional level. The participants' non-uniform lettering and limited traditional literacy skills did not stop them from taking action, from attempting to promote change. As they were learning to read words and worlds, they were attempting to rewrite their very futures, situations, and locations.

In the circle described here, the participants, women and men, engaged in problematizing salaries, something that they initially believed they could do nothing to change. Through problematizing and dialoguing about some of the issues involved, such as gender disparity in earnings, they dialogued and designed a plan of action. Participants, therefore, were becoming aware of tools they could use (problem posing, dialogue, and problem solving) to question the status quo, and to start believing in and even negotiating change. As subjects of their own learning, literants brought authentic issues to the circles and engaged in meaningful learning experiences, applicable to their everyday lives, gaining ownership of their learning.

Culture circles I observed discussed salary, employment conditions, job skills and ethics, parenting, children, education, and politics as these issues related to participants' lives. Through the exploration of relevant issues and themes, the participants posed problems, dialogued, and charted a course of action. As they problematized themes and issues, old knowledge and assumptions collided with new knowledge. Participants then deconstructed their realities and texts as they sought to reconstruct their own knowledge from a critical perspective. They became not only aware of the issues, but meta-aware. They came to recognize larger issues and institutional discourses shaping their realities. While literants engaged in naming the issue (the first step in order to promote change), they moved beyond naming to identifying larger socially, culturally, and/or historically shaped structures which shaped their realities, positioning themselves agentively.

This process happened as they shared their experiences, their perspectives, and listened to other perspectives as alternatives, as a multiplicity of angles, as explanations, collectively engaging in the critical cycle and coming to internalize many of its facets. The teacher-facilitator, Sandra, as seen in the meeting reported above, took advantage of certain moments to further the participants' queries and inquiries. She provided information, but did not necessarily dictate what went on in the circles, nor did she take the stance of teacher, as the holder of knowledge. The role of the facilitator is to facilitate and not to lead.

Critical Pedagogy Framework:
Towards *Conscientização*

Culture circles such as the one above embrace a critical or emancipatory pedagogical approach to education and aim to promote critical meta-awareness. This critical meta-awareness allows individuals and groups to engage in social action to solve problems and address issues they identify in their own narratives. This meta-awareness, or conscientization (Freire, 1970), positions them as appropriating language and not being colonized by it (Chouliaraki & Fairclough, 1999). Dialogue is the process whereby change is negotiated both at the personal and societal level. From the premise that change ought to be initiated from people's own locations in society, problem solving starts with the awareness that change can take place from the margins of society, as the margin is a vital part of the whole (hooks, 1990).

In the culture circle portrayed above, participants constantly engaged in the analysis of their own narratives. They considered multiple perspectives (both personal and institutional) and became researchers of their own situations as they analyzed narratives of livable wages, work ethics and skills, being "good mothers," and others. In the case of the analysis of the minimum wage collective narrative, participants found that the minimum wage as defined by the government was not a livable wage for a family of three, dispelling the common discourse of minimum-wage salary providing for the basic needs of a family.

Together, they subsequently planned two courses of action, one on the personal realm and another in the societal sphere. The societal plan was to make the politicians in office aware of the disparity and of the need to approve a minimum wage that truly equaled a living wage. On the personal realm, they realized that by further developing schooling skills such as literacy and problem solving they would be better prepared to take a higher paying job, therefore addressing the situated issue. This exemplifies a first step toward engaging in the concrete critical research which culture circles seek to accomplish.

While the theoretical discussion of institutional discourses is important, if we are to engage in social change, we must start by listening to and analyzing the stories common people tell, and help them to engage in this process themselves with the goal of fostering critically meta-aware individuals. By providing meaningful opportunities to engage in this process, culture circles become a site where individuals are able to distance themselves from a story to see how it is being constructed. This is a metalinguistic skill that requires insight into the power of language to mislead and/or deceive (Parmentier, 1994). "Such meta-awareness is an important life-skill...listen[ing] critically and consider[ing] life's challenges from multiple perspectives... Through reframing...narrative portrayals...[comes] aware[ness] of how the perceptions of others challenge or support their own views" (Rymes, 2001, p. 168).

Purpose of Culture Circles

The purpose of culture circles is to provide bridges to the promotion of change in oppressive situations. In the circles, literacy is approached as a tool for social change (Freire, 1998) as literants engage in critical analysis of their own tellings of institutional narratives, thereby appropriating language (Chouliaraki & Fairclough, 1999; Fairclough, 2004). More than traditionally conceived literacy, the method employed allows participants to engage in an externalization and practice of a process that lead to conscientization (Freire, 1970), to critical meta-awareness. By embracing conscientization and critical thinking, participants question the traditional discourses and problematize socially and culturally constructed concepts. Participants engage in the practice of deconstructing discourses, and learning how multiple framings can provide multiple understandings of the same issue.

As explained in Part I of the book, the process in culture circles starts with generative words and themes that emerge from its participants and the situations in which they live. Within the context of adult literacy classes in Brazil, this is important because often, prior to joining these culture circles, participants took their respective situations as their personal fate, as if there was nothing that could be done to enact change. So, the foundation and roots of these culture circles were revealed through the combination of interviews, participant observation, data collection, thematic coding (for generative themes) or corpus analysis (for generative words) and word lists generated by the teachers/facilitators. From this collecting effort, commonly cited themes and commonly used words were then contextualized in a larger context. This was accomplished by questioning the content and format of these thematic discourses.

By posing problems that served to deconstruct their very locations, participants were able to start seeing that the situations they were living were not due to fate, but to sociocultural and historical constructions and conceptions of oppression, which systematized injustices, oppressions, and prejudices. Literants engaged in collective problem posing. Posing problems about a situation previously deemed deterministic is a big step towards critical meta-awareness. By questioning the status quo, participants became aware that their lives were not externally determined and that they could choose to adopt the institutional discourse and recycle it in their narratives, living according to it. After posing a problem, they engaged in dialogue. This dialogue served to break the monological definition of their situation(s), the deterministic vein in their lives.

Within the context of culture circles, dialogue is intended to bring multiple perspectives to an issue, to empower participants, and to break down the monological expectations of what they should be and how they should live their lives. Problem solving emerges in dialogue and is geared toward action. After talking about the problem posed, participants plot a plan for action during the problem-solving stage. Action follows and may take place at the personal and/or societal level. The process is not as linear or simple as described here, as processes are hybridized and repeated according to the situation/theme being problematized. This critical cycle includes "...four components necessary for personal and group empowerment: belief in self-efficacy, validation through collective experience, knowledge and skills for critical thinking and action, and reflective action" (McNicoll, 2003, p. 46).

Internalizing this process is a way to foster the development of individual agency and action, and for these circle participants to start reinvisioning, reinventing their lives within the system or enacting change upon the structure. After all, personal and social change are dialectically related, and as such they are interactive and inseparable (Breton, 1995; Getzel, 2003).

The Theory and Practice of Culture Circles

Culture circles intend to eliminate the dichotomy between theory and practice often present in the traditional schooling environment as the practice depends on the theory and the theory depends on the practice in the implementation and maintenance of culture circles.

Looking back at my field notes, I realize how important the atmosphere of the classroom was—very conducive to dialogue. The seating arrangement contrasted traditional definitions and the banking concept of education, in which knowledge is deposited in students' heads. It allowed students to look at each other, see everyone, and value everyone's voices. There is a need to redefine discourses, knowledge, curriculum and learning for culture circles to be implemented. The somewhat unsettling element of implementing culture circles is the need to truly blur the roles of teacher and learner in a Freirean sense—the "teacher" does not know where the circle is headed. The teacher/facilitator observed and helped the group engage in meaningful dialogue. At times, this meant staying out of the way or providing minimal information. Other times, it meant bringing difficult issues to the circle or seizing moments of tension as opportunities for collective learning. While general plans were charted by facilitators, observations and everyday realities guided pedagogical actions in culture circles. No scripts were followed.

Participants in culture circles I observed were acquiring tools to articulate and pose problems, and coming up with possible solutions to their personal challenges through dialogue and problem solving.

The participants didn't necessarily find solutions to each problem, but worked towards breaking monological oppressive discourses by considering alternative perspectives, exploring multiple issues through dialogue. They became aware of some of the issues that constructed their nature and institutional identities (Gee, 2001). As some of the participants narrated, a number of them were starting to re-construct themselves, exploring the implementation of discursively constructed solutions in their lives and engaging in change enacted on the personal level. This personal action can contribute to social change over time.

Being part of these literacy-focused Brazilian culture circles allowed the literants who returned to school, after failing to succeed in formal schooling environments, to take a more agentive role, to have tools with which they might be able to promote personal change. In culture circles, participants "experience interpersonal processes with others who share their predicament of exclusion that can provide a most powerful potential for personal, interpersonal, and social change" (Shapiro, 2003, p. 19). Together, they began challenging a (mono)culturally shaped (Genishi & Goodwin, 2008) set of morals and started to collectively negotiate a new set of collective morals. This process served to illuminate the start of personal change processes.

In the circles, the participants had a chance to lay a foundation for better understanding of the process of questioning the status quo, their own current locations in society, to get a glimpse and imagine the potential for action and change on a broader scope. Such was the case of the example described earlier, in which participants in the culture circle questioned the minimum wage salary and re-imagined themselves, coming up with actions on the personal and societal levels, hints of a better future.

The Complexity of Culture Circles

Often when educators speak of Freire and literacy, they reduce the complex concept of literacy to a set of pre-scripted skills (Roberts, 2000) linked to learning how to read and write.

> Literacy education is an act of knowing,...of creating, and not the act of mechanically memorizing letters and syllables...[It] must originate from research about the vocabulary universe of the learners,...to understand culture as a human creation, an extension of the world by men and women through their work, helps to overcome the politically tragic experience of immobility caused by fatalism...Literacy education must be characterized by dialogue as a path to knowledge...[It] must be premised on remembering what it means for...adults, used to the weight of work instruments, to manipulate pencils...be premised on remembering the insecurity of illiterate adults, who will become upset if they feel they are being treated like children. There is no more effective way to respect them than to accept their experiential knowledge for the purpose of going beyond it. (Freire, 1996, pp. 128-129)

To fully implement Freire's ideas, it may be helpful to remember that he defined literacy in terms of culture (Gadotti & Romão, 2002), that students "look at themselves as persons living and producing in a given society" (Macedo & Freire, 1998, p. xi). As a result, "[w]hen men and women realize that they themselves are the makers of culture, they have accomplished...the first step toward feeling the importance, the necessity, and the possibility of owning reading and writing. They become literate, politically speaking" (p. xi), and walk towards a true democracy.

Challenging the Status Quo and Problematizing Institutional Discourses

The core of culture circles lies at the intersection of problem posing, dialogue, and problem solving. Problem posing can only take place when a person or a group sees a situation as problematic as opposed to accepting it as is and dovetailing concerns (Archer, 2003) regarding his/her/their situation. Often people experiencing oppressive situations recursively are not aware of the problems that need to be posed as they construct their own narratives.

After observing many culture circles in Brazil, I propose that the process towards change and transformation begins with the recognition and understanding that there is a process through which narrative tellings are shaped and how they come into existence. Through this process, personal events and institutional discourses are blended together in narrative tellings. Without being aware of the distinct ingredients of this mix, narrators perceive the wedding of these two to be personal beliefs shaped according to their own ideas. Instead, institutional discourse infiltrates their narratives without being questioned. Adopting institutional discourse as one's own set of beliefs and espousing them in one's narratives is one easy way to accepting their locations in society.

With the very intention of separating these perceived personal beliefs into two constituents, culture circles invite participants to engage in problem posing. The process seeks to investigate which parts of the narrative tellings are portraying institutional discourses, which parts are constructed to fit normative morals, and which parts are geared at understanding what happened (personal events). Dialogue is of paramount importance as participants try to break the seemingly monological narration of events. In circles, participants seek to recognize the infiltration of institutional discourse and challenge its absolute voice. They come to view institutional discourse as one understanding of an issue, an understanding that might actually be curtailing their agency and trapping them in a cycle of low SES and poor working conditions. As for the participants in this study, when they dropped out of school, they believed such things as "women stayed home and helped their mothers" to be the truth. Ultimately, many of them recognized traditional patriarchal discourse framing in many issues.

Culture circles encourage the problematization of its literants' situations. Communities cannot preserve their unique social identities and worldviews if they are not aware of them. Promoting social justice, therefore, often begins with cultural awareness or with conscientization efforts (Freire, 1995; Marsiglia, 2003). Fostering the appropriation of discourse, the understanding of discourses as framed a particular way, circles seek to counter the all too common colonization—the maintenance of oppressive structures, such as the ones keeping low-SES women in rural areas from being formally schooled. The process seeks to promote dialogue aimed at deconstructing narrative tellings.

Replacing perceived personal beliefs with internal conversation (individually) or dialogue (collectively) allows participants to deconstruct narrative tellings into their basic components, identifying the institutional discourses infiltrating their narratives; to question some previously conceived universal truths, facts. This process explicitly outlined in culture circle settings models the process of internal conversation. Seeking to teach adults how to read, circles also provide literants with tools to engage in the critical analysis of their narratives and situations, therefore giving them tools to enact agency at an individual level.

Culture circles foster not only the teaching of reading and writing, but higher-order skills, such as problem solving. This process goes from deconstruction to constructivism. From this perspective, language is not representational, or even relevantly systematic, and therefore it is potentially colonizing. Even the structural, grammatical regularities of language are infinitely manipulated so that their ability to represent is reduced to mere play at best or, ideological confusion at worst. The role of culture circles and the process it fosters, then, is to uncover this ideological component—so that people will not be taken in by it. The constructivist, building his or her own resistant analysis, rises from the deconstructed ashes generated by the process of problem posing and dialogue.

CHAPTER 5

Culture Circles in
Pre-Service Teacher Education

Being a teacher today is no easy matter. Increasing demands on teachers, including larger classes, pressures to follow rigid standardized curriculum and "teach to the test," and decreased support for public education, result in pressure cooker schools that are unengaging for both teachers and students. Sadly, many teachers fall victim to the challenges of teaching, especially new teachers in urban schools, about half of whom leave the profession within five years.

Nieto (2007, p. xi)

As a teacher educator, I feel great responsibility as I seek to prepare new teachers for diverse classrooms and support them once they enter "pressure cooker schools." Nevertheless, I know that I do not have all the answers. As I teach pre-service teachers, we embark on a learning journey. We simultaneously occupy roles of teachers and learners and grow in the process. Together, we negotiate what it means to be a teacher-learner, a reflective and transformative practitioner. We link theory and practice. We theorize from our very practices, from our practicums and student teaching experiences. In this chapter, I share ways in which I employed

Freirean culture circles in educating pre-service teachers in an early childhood education program in an American university.

The Problem of Traditional Models of Pre-Service Teacher Education

Throughout the country, traditional models of pre-service teacher education focus on teaching methods and curriculum implementation (Hughes, 1999). This is done via a model which focuses on the transmission and mastery of knowledge, based on a banking concept of education (Freire, 1970). This reality is evidenced by the ways academic degree programs are designed—grounded in social studies, science, mathematics, and language and literacy methods which are then brought together in a curriculum integration course (Anderson, 2005).

In teacher preparation programs, future teachers learn about so-called "best" practices, implementing curricula, and teaching strategies. When comparing teacher education programs from 20 universities in the United States (Souto-Manning, Cahnmann-Taylor, Dice, & Wooten, 2008), we found that programs were mostly organized around content areas and that methods courses focused on giving teachers the tools to meet curricular standards and cover content. Little time was spent focusing on ways to teach individual children in classrooms and to build upon their interests, experiences, and strengths. As a result, many current teacher education programs seem to leave new teachers unprepared for the possibility of clashing educational paradigms, childrearing beliefs, and personal characteristics (Cochran-Smith & Lytle, 1990; Cannella & Reiff, 1994; Darling-Hammond, 2000). Figure 5.1 (below) illustrates our findings regarding the common structure of early childhood teacher education programs leading to initial certification in the U.S.

As portrayed in Figure 5.1 and documented by many researchers (Porfilio and Yu, 2006; Tom, 1997), teacher education programs leading to initial certification in early childhood education are very top-down and solution oriented. They are based on monologues—

professors are perceived as the holders of knowledge that must be mastered by students in order to become competent early childhood educators. Curricula and syllabi revolve around traditionally defined texts, which often become the voice of authority. Finally, this model culminates in catharsis, as pre-service teachers feel a sense of relief and do away with the stress associated with not knowing what to do. This catharsis comes as a result of having found "the answer" to a situation.

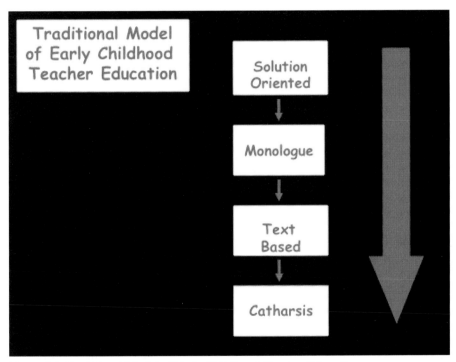

Figure 5.1. Traditional Model of Early Childhood Teacher Education (Souto-Manning et al., 2008)

By adhering to such models, new teachers come to rely on as-signed texts and classroom discussions and accept a subtle message that there is a specific protocol or procedure for each situation (Coch-ran-Smith & Fries, 2001). Nevertheless, these "solutions" often do not work across time and space, or at least not as they were intended.

They embody the idea of "best" practices, which are (mono)culturally shaped (Genishi & Goodwin, 2008) and honor certain cultural practices to the detriment of others, refuting the true meaning of critical multicultural education. Nowhere do pre-service teachers have the experience of active social engagement (Rhedding-Jones, 2002; Rust, 1999). Rather, despite concern that students become familiar with issues of multiculturalism, in the typical program their experience is too often text based; students read and discuss discrimination based on race, class, gender and other social oppressions through a professor-assigned text.

Conversely, culture circles refute the idea of a specific protocol for each situation, challenge text-based, single-answer approaches to dealing with oppressive situations, and present an empowering way to question the status quo through active social engagement on personal and societal realms. As LeAnn, a pre-service teacher in my class voiced:

> I know that sometimes I leave this class with more questions than answers. But if I am to be a reflective teacher, I need to think, to rethink, to do, to redo, and to learn in the process. Thinking about the whys and pushing back together is what we do. I know it is okay not to know everything...This process has helped me so much—What is the issue? How's this happening? Why? Together, we talk about the issues, we talk, we listen and we learn. We come up with possible ways of changing things. This helped me see how teachers are change agents. I invite the children to ask why, 'cuz they can change the world. They are our hope for tomorrow.

The Need for Critical Multicultural Teacher Education

According to Dorothy Nolte (1998), "children learn what they live" (p. vi). They learn by experiencing the world, by living situations. So, if we, multicultural educators and teacher educators, want children to embrace critical practices and stances, we need to promote liberatory pedagogical practices in the teacher education classroom. This is because adults also learn experientially—by doing. According to James (1980):

> ...educators are apt to follow John Dewey's notion that the challenge of any form of education is to select present experiences that will live fruitfully and creatively in future experience. Few would disagree with this. Dewey, who was probably the greatest educational thinker ever produced in this country, wrote of learning as an experiential continuum, a continuity of growth experiences. But here is where the disagreement begins, because he characterized learning not as the experience itself, but as thinking about experience. So a form of education...that provides intense experiences also needs to provide tools for thinking about those experiences, for tying what has happened on a course into the experiential continuum of those who have passed through it.

I would go further and say that the challenge of education is to consider access, equity, and power and embrace liberatory, transformative pedagogical practices. The challenge is then not to create master texts or intense experiences, but to develop (or adapt) pedagogical processes which can honor situated contexts and promote authentic forums for problematization, dialogue, and transformation. In this way, instead of living (or leading, if you will) by example, by reading what a person has done, by learning about the answers one has found, educators can embrace the tasks of re-creating a pedagogy (such as the one in culture circles) in their own contexts.

The curriculum of culture circles emerges from the pre-service teachers' experiences and builds upon them. As another participant in pre-service teacher education culture circles, Saundra, voiced:

> Everything we learn is relevant to our situation, to our teaching. I don't have to sit through and think how this and that have nothing to do with what I'm living in the classroom. What we are learning comes from what we are living. If we are struggling to deal with our belief about African American English because we grew up thinking it was wrong, we talk about Englishes in the classroom. We can't build on students' strengths if we don't really see their strengths. So, we talk about the issues. We learn about the structure of African American English, why we grew up

thinking it was wrong—or talking two ways, one at school and one at home. We don't have to be ashamed or afraid to sound dumb. There are no dumb questions. We talk about all those things that are iffy, edgy, things that we cannot talk about anywhere else, but that affect the children we are teaching, their lives. The way this class is set up, it's a safe space, a space for us to say I don't know, to say, yes, I am a teacher and a learner. I don't have to know it all, but I can't justify unjust actions by not knowing. I know I am accountable and that ignorance is no excuse for committing injustices. I know that I can feel supported, but at the same time pushed to rethink what I am doing, again and again.

To embrace equality in education, educators engage in critical, transformative, multicultural education, and collectively and dialectically challenge and change models and beliefs that position diverse people as having deficits, as lacking something. Acknowledging that all learning is influenced by cultural differences and by the context in which it takes place we engage in collective learning, thereby forming a socially mediated community of diverse educators (Nieto, 1999, p. 3) committed to equity and excellence. As a teacher educator seeking to support and expand the belief that all individuals have strengths and that we can all learn from each other, I engaged in multicultural teacher education that is critical, transformative, actively and dynamically constructed, from the ground up. I employed Freirean culture circles in the pre-service teacher education classroom.

Culture Circles and Multicultural Education

Multicultural education is an imperative in the 21st century in light of the "nation's deepening ethnic texture, interracial tension and conflict" (Banks, 2007, p. xi). Multicultural education in the U.S. emerged during the civil rights movement of the 1960s and 1970s (Banks, 1995). Until then, it was widely accepted that diverse people were either inferior or culturally deprived (Goodwin, Cheruvu, & Genishi, 2008), hence the separation of schools according to race and the funding of programs to provide a "head start" to children who did not have fit or proper homes. Multicultural education focuses on challenging these ideas that saw diverse individuals in terms of deficits (as lacking something or needing to be fixed) or as inferior. James Banks (1995) explained that the goal of multicultural education is "to reform the school and other educational institutions so that students from diverse racial, ethnic and social-class groups will experience educational equity" (p. 3).

Sonia Nieto (2002) wrote that:

Multicultural education...challenges and rejects racism and other forms of discrimination in schools and society and accepts and affirms the pluralism (ethnic, racial, linguistic, religious, economic, and gender, among others) that students, their communities, and teachers reflect. Multicultural education permeates...interactions among teachers, students, and families, and the very way that schools conceptualize the nature of teaching and learning. Because it uses critical pedagogy as its underlying philosophy and focuses on knowledge, reflection, and action (praxis) as the basis for social change, multicultural education promotes democratic principles of social justice. (pp. 29-30)

Multicultural education seeks to support a diversities perspective (Carter & Goodwin, 1994), expanding the affirmation of diversities as an essential attribute of a democratic society (Nieto, 2000). Furthermore, multicultural education seeks to respect the humanity of every person, prioritizing teachers' and students' personal, practical knowledge as foundational to promoting change in teaching and teacher education. It proposes that we must begin to appreciate that "each is unique in their walking of this earth, each an entire universe, each somehow sacred. This recognition...demands that we embrace the humanity of every student" (Ayers, 2004, p. 35).

Banks & Banks (2004) defined multicultural education as "a field of study designed to increase educational equity for all students that incorporates, for this purpose, content, concepts, principles, theories, and paradigms from history, the social behavioral sciences, and particularly from ethnic studies and women's studies" (p. xii). According to Banks (2007), multicultural education aims "to improve race relations and to help all students acquire the knowledge, attitudes and skills needed to participate in cross-cultural interactions and in personal, social, and civic action that will help make our nation more democratic and just" (p. xii). Banks (2004) developed five dimensions of multicultural education:

- *content integration* (using multiple cultural perspectives, knowledges, and experiences when teaching concepts and skills);
- *knowledge construction process* (locating the sociocultural and historical construction of knowledge);
- *prejudice reduction* (helping students develop positive cross-cultural and intergroup attitudes and actions);
- *equity pedagogy* (implementing teaching strategies that honor multiple groups—in terms of race, class, culture, etc.); and
- *empowering school culture and social structure* (changing the status of diverse groups in school, fostering an equitable experience in terms of power and status).

To implement multicultural teacher education, educators must focus on implementing these five dimensions (Banks, 2004; 2007).

Culture circles provide fertile grounds for multicultural education. This is because the pedagogy employed in the circles embodies a pedagogical practice which considers a variety of perspectives and knowledges while honoring situated experiences through generative themes. It locates the sociocultural and historical contexts and discourses shaping everyday situations, and embraces dialogue which honors multiple viewpoints and backgrounds. Finally, through problem solving and action, culture circle participants engage in collective actions and strive to foster more equitable experiences. Thus, culture circle pedagogy meets all the dimensions established by James Banks (2004; 2007) as requisite conditions for multicultural education.

Doing Multicultural
Teacher Education through Culture Circles

Fennimore (2000) and Hoffman (1996) noted that little is truly known about how to do multiculturalism in schools. As pre-service teachers and I sought to engage in critical multicultural teacher education, we wanted to make sure not to fall into the trivialized and decontextualized infusion of cultural celebrations while ignoring the everyday issues and tensions experienced by diverse teachers in their everyday lives. Instead of thinking of teachers in terms of what they were not able to do in their classrooms (in terms of deficits), I wanted to engage pre-service teachers in a rich multicultural experience that empowered them to understand themselves in relation to others.

I wanted to instill in pre-service teachers the awareness of their ability to change oppressive, unjust relationships. Further, I wanted to nurture their desire to change educational practices and relationships and challenge deficit perceptions of minority children. Together, we engaged in the negotiation of our struggles with colleagues, administrators, parents or students. Engaging in culture circles in pre-service teacher education would then allow these soon-to-be teachers to envision and embrace the necessity to promote change.

Generative Themes: Practical Knowledge as Foundation to Critical Education

In order to engage in critical education, I believe that teacher educators need to prioritize teachers' personal, practical knowledge as foundational to critical, multicultural reflection on power, identity and professional struggle in education (c.f. Shulman & Mesa-Bains, 1993; Gomez & Abt-Perkins, 1995; Gomez, 2002). By positioning myself as an ethnographer, collecting data as I observed and supervised 22 practicum and student teaching placements over a semester, I was able to bring in experiences relevant to the university classroom. After collecting data (notes, recordings, artifacts, interviews), I codified students' experiences of recurring struggle. I brought generative themes to the classroom in the codified form of vignettes, videos, picture books, and photos.

This practice allowed me to publicly acknowledge that there are cultural ways of learning and that there are multiple discontinuities or mismatches between home and school, or between one's culture and the culture of school (Moll, Amanti, Neff, & Gonzalez, 1992; Purcell-Gates, 1995). For example, I noticed that pre-service teachers were most familiar in settings that mirrored their own schooling experiences. Consequently, speakers of mainsteam American English (MAE) were most comfortable in settings in which MAE was spoken. Becoming aware of this and bringing it to the class allowed many of the pre-service teachers to recognize why they did not like their placement setting or why they felt uncomfortable or inadequate.

Together, we talked about how individuals engage in culturally specific ways of talking, teaching, and learning. "Culture does not exist in a vacuum but rather is situated in particular historical, social, political, and economic conditions" (Nieto, 2002, p. 11). We engaged in an inquiry and found that many researchers have documented cultural specificities (Valdés, 1996; Cazden, 1986; Heath, 1983) contributing to our knowledge base. This allowed us to recognize that we needed to learn more about embracing other cultures as opposed to measuring them against our own primary cultural practices. We came to the realization that if we were going to engage in genuine multicultural education, we needed to pay attention to the individual experiences of people as opposed to drawing on stereotypes and large generalizations. Marianne voiced:

> You know, I always thought that the challenge was that Black people did not have the opportunities at home, but now I know that it is because what is taught at school is different from the way they live at home. Or maybe, you know, because families are different. But imagine entering the classroom and being told that the way you lived, the way you talk, the way you are, are not good enough. Imagine how miserable a kid is when he enters a classroom and is told to act White. I feel I have so much to learn. I

don't know much about African American families or African American English, but I want to learn.

Problematizing: Asking Why and How This Had Come into Being

In problematizing the situation, the pre-service teachers asked why and how this cultural mismatch had come into being.

Carry: And why does this happen?

Mariana: What?

Carry: How can teachers get away with treating their students this way?

Mariana: Well, many may not even notice. Naming the issue, recognizing it is the first step.

Moesha: Yeah, and it's better than it used to be. My grandma went to them Black schools that don' have no new books, jus' old ones. You know, now children are in the same schools.

Hilda: Yeah, but it doesn't make it right.

Destiny: Look around. How many teachers are White? How many of us are White? It's about the culture of the teacher. The teacher is the knower, right? If the teacher is the knower and the teacher is White, schooling is White, knowledge is White.

Carry: I don't agree with this. I am White and I don't think this way.

Stephanie: Yeah, this is what we can do, Carry. We can change things. We don't have to be teaching in our cultural ways, we need to see that there are many cultures in the classroom.

Hilda: And we can be teachers who are learners.

Destiny: We need to talk, to ask why, to change things.

Allie: We can ask the questions. We can be real advocates for our students.

Hilda: But how do we know?

Berry: How can we learn?

Together, we read studies that had documented mismatch in communicative actions. These studies informed our dialogues and the ways in which we started negotiating change through collective problem solving. We used the texts to inform our learning, but not as providing canned responses to the specific situations that pre-service teachers were experiencing. For example, together we talked about how Guadalupe Valdés (1996) reported the discontinuity between the home and school worlds of Latino children due to mismatch of cultural contexts. We also talked about how Courtney Cazden (1986) pinpointed the different ways of speaking and telling stories, teaching and learning across home and school contexts. Further, we read Shirley Brice Heath's study (1983) of a community in the Carolina Piedmont which found that children in three neighboring communities had very specific ways of speaking and interacting that were particular to the communities in which they lived. Together, we examined how in one of the communities there were very rich oral traditions (storytelling, analogies, group interactions) and book reading was not common. In another, book knowledge was highly valued, so there was a lot of non-fiction book reading but not a lot of fiction reading; stretching and applying the knowledge and ideas exposed in the books were largely absent. In yet another community, literacy practices closely resembled school literacy practices. Children in this third community were most successful in school. What this told us was that we were not truly infusing multicultural practices in schools, but honoring a (mono)cultural practice (Genishi & Goodwin, 2008). Multicultural education is antiracist, basic, and important for all students (Nieto, 2002). It is a process grounded on critical pedagogy. The classroom dialogue continued:

Hilda: If these books were written so long ago, why are children still being blamed for talking their way?
Destiny: That's right.
Mariana: Change takes time. It's easier to keep going.
Allie: But we don't have the time. Time could mean failing children. It does.

LeAnn: We can start change in our own classroom. We can learn about our children's traditions and honor them.

Moesha: But we have to be careful not to fail these children by tellin' them they can be talking their own way. They need to know how to talk the school talk too. Cuz when I wrote my application essay, I didn't write in no African American English or they'd think I could not do school work and get good grades.

Destiny: Uh-hum.

The section of the dialogue presented above illustrates the pre-service teachers' frustration with the lack of connection between these powerful studies and the practices they saw in early educational settings. Not all, but many settings treated children from culturally and linguistically diverse backgrounds as culturally deprived and needing to be fixed.

Through problematizing the status quo, becoming aware of multicultural issues and the privileging of White middle class ways of knowing while wanting to honor the experiences of diverse children and families, these pre-service teachers started examining the ways that racism is enacted across institutions and in everyday life (Gillborn, 2006; Ladson-Billings & Tate, 1995). They began reflecting and focusing on their own educational experiences and the classrooms where they were placed for practica and student teaching.

Towards Dialogic Problem Solving and Action

In the teacher education classroom, our dialogue purposefully sought to forefront the voices and narrative realities of people who experienced oppression, highlighting the lived experiences of racism with the potential of exposing everyday, unexamined racist assumptions that permeate our lives, thereby helping others understand how race is inextricably tied to daily life (Ladson-Billings, 2004).

LeAnn: When he speaks in African American English, he gets corrected and then he gets so frustrated he throws a fit. He knows his teacher understands him, but how he's saying is more important than what he's saying, at least in the classroom.

Moesha: I know what you mean, cuz I lived it. I'd not speak up. When I did, I got corrected. I looked dumb. I hated it.

Allie: In my classroom, in Head Start, the children are going to school for the first time. They get there, and, you know, they are anxious about leaving their mommies, and all of them are African American and the teachers are White, and then, they can't speak right. It breaks my heart. It's not that the teachers are mean. They believe that they are doing the best for the children.

Destiny: So, you know, teachers say that they don't see color. But when children enter the classroom, three-year-olds, their first experience with school, and they are told how to speak right, then you know that this talk about race not having anything to do with their experience, with their lives is nonsense.

Documenting, problematizing, and dialoguing together about the experiences of children of color in early education, we confirmed that inside public schools and federally funded programs, the colonization of people of color continues. Vivid experiences and culturally relevant knowledge brought to school are negated by the official school curriculum at structural and institutional levels (Nieto, 2002; Villenas & Deyhle, 1999). While educational settings such as schools and early educational programs claim to be objective "culture-free" zones, through our critical analysis of situated incidents, it became clear that most continue to be institutions that favor White middle-class cultures and discourses (Grant & Sleeter, 1996).

We talked about how not examining the privileging of White middle-class culture in schools is problematic and discussed the role of race in curriculum, instruction, assessment, and school funding in the failure of schools. We went on to recognize (in our own settings and in published studies documenting multiple instances of this phenomenon throughout the country) the academic advantages afforded to White, middle-class students (Ladson-Billings, 2004). We came to analyze our own privileges and realized that in order to grow as a nation, to rethink and do diversities in early childhood education (Genishi & Goodwin, 2008), there is a continued need to understand the nuances of racialized practices within school settings and how Whiteness "manifests and affects schooling in tangible ways, such as setting standards for 'normal' and 'acceptable' actions" (Rogers & Mosley, 2006, p. 465).

Through culture circles, we uncovered the fact that when the subtext of these racialized and discriminatory discourses and actions were problematized, acts of White supremacy came to the surface and were "seen to relate to the operation of forces that saturate the everyday, mundane actions and policies that shape the world in the interest of White people" (Gillborn, 2006, p. 174). Thus the ways in which teachers are positioned moment to moment in the classroom, how they negotiate relationships with students and families, and the effects of such practices over time are linked to these discourses and actions. If teachers do not stop to think about privilege and access, they are accepting their position of power and forcing their cultural views and practices onto others as "best" practices. When teachers ask "best for whom?" they start uncovering the cultural nature of discourses that shape the field, such as developmentally appropriate practices (Bredekamp & Copple, 2009) and "best" practices.

For example, one of the tensions brought to the teacher education classroom through generative themes was that in this era of raising standards and meeting adequate yearly progress as mandated by *No Child Left Behind*, many schools place insurmountable amounts of pressure and stress on teachers in order to prove that students are indeed making academic progress. By problematizing this issue, we uncovered the sociocultural and historical forces shaping this so-called "accountability system." Through problematization and dialogic problem solving, pre-service teachers discovered that students are segregated in schools and the lowest levels become the dumping ground for minority students while White middle-class students are provided with enrichment activities such as gifted programs (Codron, 2007; Gillborn, 2005). Hence segregation continues to exist in schools. As a result, tensions and stresses are experienced by teachers day in and day out.

While we did not often engage in transformative action as a result of culture circles in my pre-service teacher education classroom, I propose that by carefully documenting and critiquing what was currently happening in education, matters of race and inequality could be problematized through authentic, critical dialogue. Pre-service teachers shared their observations with collaborating teachers, thereby engaging in raising awareness for all involved. Some of the time, the pre-service teachers' actions were disregarded, but other times, their action of naming an issue made collaborating teachers aware of the misalignment of school and home cultures. In class, by problematizing issues of inequity dialogically, pre-service teachers sought to uncover the larger discourses and institutional forces influencing schools, they came to see schools as part of (and as a mirror image of) society. Together, we tried to strategize and collectively envision ways in which they could contribute towards changing these situations.

The Role of the Teacher Educator

As a teacher educator committed to social justice, I wanted to use the teacher education classroom space to facilitate and promote change. I believe that if pre-service teachers investigate recurring oppressions experienced by the children that inhabited their student teaching and practica placements, by their mentor teachers, and by themselves (pre-service teachers), they will likely feel compelled to problem solve and take action. By engaging in such a process whereby oppressions and isms are named, problematized, and challenged dialogically, teacher educators can help pre-service teachers move towards challenging the separate and unequal atmosphere experienced by diverse children. But, what is the role of the teacher educator in this process? While I cannot generalize here, I can share my role in the process.

I saw my role as a learner and as a facilitator, as someone who could create a safe environment for a community of learners who would in turn critically examine the world while striving to change it. In a Freirean way, my intention for us was to read the world together, undressing layer after layer of injustice. So, while I offered the comfort of a safe place, I also pushed these pre-service teachers to look at the realities and acknowledge many injustices the children they were teaching were experiencing. I wanted my students to make difference visible, even if it had been part of their lives for so long that they had come to accept it as a given, as a common practice. I wanted them to pose problems, to question, to dare. In so doing, I initially had a sad and depressed group of pre-service teachers. Acknowledging that many teachers feel powerless and many families feel hopeless, I sought to move them from a pedagogy of indignation (which propelled them to do something about the injustices) towards a pedagogy of hope (in which they could envision ways to change these unjust situations).

Together, we engaged in dialogue about what could be done. We did not have all the answers, but found strengths and perspectives in each other. We researched and inquired into the histories of situations that were affecting the everyday lives of the classrooms we inhabited. We came to recognize that together we were more than the sum of our individual actions.

Being a teacher educator and employing culture circle pedagogy initially meant that I positioned myself as an ethnographer. I spent lots of time documenting the culture and events of the classrooms at four school sites where my 22 students were placed. While this was not necessarily ideal, it was manageable. Each classroom had at least two interns, so I was documenting situations in about 12 classrooms, collecting data, looking for themes across settings and phenomena across situated contexts which were relevant to most (if not all) pre-service teachers. As the semester progressed, students started observing and coding situations themselves and bringing in generative themes to the classroom. Some of the thematization and codification happened outside of the teacher education classroom in more informal settings. Sometimes, pre-service teachers would contact me and let me know what they were noticing and I would codify their experiences. Halfway through the semester, they started codifying those experiences themselves. This shift happened as I started paying less attention to the culture of the classrooms and more attention to the pre-service teachers' experiences and performance. So, while it may appear to result in an insurmountable amount of work, it was manageable.

As a teacher educator, exploring multicultural teacher education through culture circles enabled me to look at specific situations and stories while shedding light onto others. This kind of multicultural teacher education frees teachers "from stereotypes concerning the groups to which they belong, [and] can open many possibilities..." (Fennimore, 2000, p. 89). In the process, I wanted not only to make teachers aware of multiple cultures, backgrounds and ways of being, but also to encourage change in a critical way. Joe Kincheloe and Peter McLaren (2005) wrote that criticality is constantly being reenvisioned. As we learned more, we reformed our theories and definitions. Seeking to know more while not focusing on how pre-service teachers, children, and their mentor teachers negotiated stresses, but rather starting from their specific stories allowed us to avoid stereotyping individuals. As I sought to inspire my pre-service teachers to embrace the role of critical learners, continuously reenvisioning the process, I did the same. I sought to raise awareness of collective struggles and encourage change. Pat Hill Collins (2000) wrote that consciousness is "continually evolving and negotiated" (p. 285). This critical consciousness (*conscientização*), according to Freire (1971) is:

> an act of knowing, if our understanding of this act is a dialectical one. Therefore, *conscientização* cannot be either an act of transference of knowledge, nor an intellectual game, but rather...an act of knowing that demands praxis...[T]he process of *conscientização* which does not pass through the unveiling of reality to the practice of its transformation, is a process which becomes frustrated. (p. 4)

Allocating time, space, and tools for envisioning change in what is so often a threatening and unfriendly environment was, in my experience, extremely important in evolving and negotiating consciousness, in doing multicultural teacher education, in exploring the ways in which people could be both oppressed and oppressor at the same time (Boal, 1995). After all, according to Nieto (2002), "learning is not simply a matter of transmitting knowledge, but rather of working with students so that they can reflect, theorize, and create knowledge" (p. 7). In educating teachers, then, teacher educators need to continuously remind ourselves to provide opportunities for students to create and re-create their ideas and realities.

The pre-service teachers and I found that often deficit-based images of students were bestowed upon them by a systemic discourse of readiness—who is ready for school, who is ready for the next grade level, who is ready to succeed—all of which are based on a White middle-class discourse and definition of success in schooling (Gee, 1996). Many teachers and administrators often bought into such ideas and discourses without questioning them or challenging their sociocultural and historical construction. I know that every day, pre-service teachers encounter many deficit-based practices. Such encounters may be tense, but they can also open up possibilities for change, activism, and advocacy if pre-service teachers have access to critical, transformative pedagogies. According to Nieto (2002), when students' "skills and knowledge are dismissed as inappropriate for the school setting, schools lose a golden opportunity to build on their students' lives in the service of their learning" (pp. 9-10). In such a vein, developing these critical, transformative pedagogies in teacher education programs via the use of culture circles is a powerful way of creating multicultural learning communities for teachers. Hopefully, these communities will become a catalyst for change and these students will become stewards of social justice.

The Power of Doing Multicultural Education through Culture Circles

No teacher education program can prepare teachers for diverse class-rooms and communities unless it is grounded on multicultural educa-tion. "The alternative to multicultural education is *monocultural education*" (Nieto, 2002, p. 36), which further reinforces the dominant culture prevalent in U.S. schools. When teachers receive pre-service and in-service training and preparation based on monocultural education, they are at best miseducated. Multicultural education should be integral to all teacher education programs, as it is

> a philosophy, a way of looking at the world, not simply a program or a class or a teacher...All good education connects theory with reflection and action...Developing a multicultural perspective means learning how to think in more inclusive and expansive ways, reflecting on what we learn, and applying the learning to real situations...Multicultural education invites students and teachers to put their learning into action for social justice." (Nieto, 2002, pp. 39-40)

Sonia Nieto has documented the power of collective reflection as a process, sharing the stories of teachers about why they teach (2005). She has masterfully pinpointed what keeps teachers going (2003) in spite of the many difficulties, stresses, and tensions they experience everyday. Building on this insightful work, I find that Freirean culture circles can serve as a powerful method, playing a paramount role in creating change, in promoting teacher education for social justice, focusing on personal and practical knowledge. After all, "it is no longer possible to separate learning from the context in which it takes place, nor from an understanding of how culture and society influence and are influenced by learning" (Nieto, 2002, p. 16).

Culture Circles as a Paradigm for Resistance and Transformation

In educating future teachers for diversity, I employed the critical cycle inherent in culture circles. Culture circles embodied multicultural teacher education as a way of resisting the dominant models of schooling. Geneva Gay (1995) pinpointed the common issues that multicultural education and critical pedagogy tackle, coming to label them as "mirror images." I prioritized teachers' personal, practical knowledge because "[t]he most successful education is that which begins with the learner and, when using a multicultural perspective...[teachers] themselves become the foundation for the [teacher education] curriculum" (Nieto, 2002, p. 46). Thus, there exists a perfect fit between culture circles and critical pedagogy for promoting multicultural education.

Culture circles embrace generative data sets, which, according to Linda Darling-Hammond (2006), are a necessity to engage in multicultural teacher education. Stories that shape the curriculum in teacher education must be generated in the classroom, from real interactions. Accessing the resources pre-service teachers bring to the teacher education classroom is fundamental to engage in critical multicultural teacher education. "The clear exposition of how teachers [and teacher educators] can assemble such cultural data sets and the practice that draws upon them is a tremendous contribution to teacher education" (p. xx).

I hope that my experience of employing culture circles in pre-service teacher education will prompt you to recreate this pedagogy in your own context, fostering the development of teachers' abilities to see beyond their individual perspectives, "to put oneself in the shoes of the learner and to understand the meaning of that experience in terms of learning...perhaps the most important role of teacher preparation" (Darling-Hammond, 2006) and of true multicultural education.

CHAPTER 6

Culture Circles in
In-Service Teacher Education

A critical teacher education as it problematizes knowledge distances itself from
that which can be easily known. In this way, the teacher education advocated
here brings students to a place they may never have been before in higher
education: a terrain of discomfort where knowledge is too complex to simply
give it out...

Kincheloe (2005, p. 101)

When I taught primary grades in an American public elementary school, I was regularly part of professional development sessions and workshops. I often resented going to
these in-service events. This resentment was not due to the fact that I
did not want to learn. I did. As a teacher, I was committed to being a
lifelong learner. Nevertheless, I resented these sessions because I felt
they were a poor attempt at framing teachers as lifelong learners.
Typically someone who was not familiar with the realities of my
classroom and school was telling me what to do—without knowing
who I was, how I was teaching, and who my students were.

According to the many comments made by teachers in the school where I taught, the general attitude towards professional development was that it was inconvenient. Colleagues often voiced their views that it was something that they had to endure, or simply put, a waste of our time. It was a time for us to hear about all that we should be doing (and assumedly were not). The assumption that our classrooms lacked these promising practices was problematic, as it framed teachers in terms of deficits and classroom instruction in need of fixing (Carter & Goodwin, 1994).

As I became a teacher educator, I was determined to challenge and change the landscape of in-service teacher education. I wanted to confront the perception that professional development sessions were conducted by university professors (or people with advanced degrees or corporate backing) who would tell teachers all they should be doing without acknowledging the everyday realities, accomplishments, challenges, and constraints experienced by teachers. To do so, I decided to engage in Freirean culture circles with early childhood teachers, investigating this liberatory, critical framework as a way to rethink, to reimagine, to transform teacher education.

I believed that Freirean culture circles would allow me to join teachers in the process of reading, writing (and rewriting) their worlds. Culture circles would provide a framework for professional development to be generative, to emerge from teachers' practices and realities. Furthermore, it would provide educators tools to challenge and change situations.

A Generative Approach to Professional Development

Teacher culture circles are a generative approach to professional development. Such an approach to in-service teacher education honors teachers' background experiences and knowledge as well as what they are already doing in their classrooms, thereby building on their strengths. It is generative because themes discussed and issues addressed are generated from the teachers' experiences and struggles.

This kind of professional development employs Freirean pedagogy (Freire, 1970) which proposes that social interaction mediates the learning process (Berk & Winsler, 1995). It begins with the assumption that "action is mediated and cannot be separated from the milieu in which it is carried out" (Wertsch, 1991, p. 18).

At the heart of teacher culture circles is the belief that teachers bring a wealth of practices, experiences, and knowledge with them. Thus teachers and teacher educators learn from each other and navigate the roles of teacher and learner dynamically and symbiotically. Such an approach frames teachers as active subjects and refutes the model of teachers as recipients of "best practices." By engaging in the critical cycle, teachers problem-pose, dialogue, and problem-solve collectively. They critically construct new bodies of knowledge which honor multiple cultural resources and legacies, leading to transformative action.

Teacher culture circles are reflective in nature because the process starts with data from teachers' classrooms and aims to promote action. Additionally, this generative approach to professional development considers individual characteristics and interests, as it is an applied approach to in-service teacher education. It is an ongoing process intended to be continued over many meetings.

A Situated Representation of Teacher Culture Circles

In 2006, as an early childhood teacher educator in an American Institution of Higher Education, I decided to engage in generative, Freirean professional development. I realized that affecting early educational settings to become more culturally responsive required the ability to communicate through conflict and consider multiple perspectives, breaking down barriers to social change. I believed that the critical cycle inherent to culture circles would allow teachers to collectively re-envision early education in their own settings, considering multiple perspectives and cultural practices.

I wanted to focus on working with early childhood teachers, as they are often not seen as "true professionals" (Johansson, 2006). Often these teachers work longer hours, are paid less than K-12 teachers, and are seen as babysitters by employers as well as the families they serve. Seeking to challenge such a location, I invited early childhood teachers educating children birth to age five in a university-affiliated preschool to join me to learn more about early literacy practices.

The university-affiliated preschool where this teacher culture circle took place was small. It consisted of seven classrooms each with lead and assistant teachers. It served a population of around 120 children, of which one-third were at or below the federally established poverty line. The percentage of children of color was about 40%. Of the children who were above the poverty line, many came from families in which parents held advanced degrees and earned six-digit annual household incomes. The county in which this preschool was located had been identified as one of the ten persistently poorest counties with populations of over 100,000 inhabitants in the United States. While the preschool served a diverse population, its student body did not mirror the county's socioeconomic landscape. The preschool functioned from 7:30 am to 5:30 pm year-round, closing for a period of two weeks in December and another period of two weeks in July. Lead teachers in this preschool held bachelors or advanced degrees related to early education and child development. Assistant teachers held a CDA credential (Child Development Associate) or its equivalent. NAEYC (National Association for the Education of Young Children) recommended ratios were closely implemented and monitored. Creative Curriculum™ (http://www.creativecurriculum.net/) was adopted school-wide.

The in-service teacher culture circle I discuss in this chapter met between the months of August 2006 to July 2008. Every other week, eight teachers and I met to problematize everyday issues and engage in dialogic, collective, critical learning processes. During this time, as the culture circle facilitator, I engaged in ethnographic observations (field notes, video and audio recordings, interviews, artifacts) of participating teachers' classrooms and of our own culture circle in order to learn from the process. In doing so, I aimed to document the situated representation of transformative teacher education (Dyson & Genishi, 2005)—a critical teacher study group.

In implementing Freirean culture circles in teacher education, I wanted to explore how early childhood teachers engaged in dialogue through differences of perspective (Genishi & Goodwin, 2008). In doing so, I reframed my role as teacher educator, becoming both an ethnographer (Moll et al., 1992) and an action researcher. I documented relevant themes generating from the teachers' classrooms and facilitated the teacher culture circle. Together, we embraced teacher education as a process of problem posing (Freire, 1970). We sought to uncover, problematize, and change issues that were common yet often ignored in the everyday lives of early childhood teachers, such as the isolation inherent in the teaching profession (Rogers & Babinski, 2002).

In documenting the process over time, I wanted to learn about the power and possibilities of teacher culture circles, focusing on how the process happened and its potential for transformative action. Furthermore, I wanted to assess if and in what ways participation in a teacher culture circle propelled change and transformation in the lives of its participants.

Early Literacy: A Generative Theme as an Invitation

We started by addressing issues of early literacy. The focus on early literacy was purposeful. As a former primary grades teacher, I had experienced a push-down of traditional literacy practices. Celia Genishi and Anne Haas Dyson (2009) documented that starting "in kindergarten, there is often a stark curricular shift" signaled by "prescribed literacy focused curricula" (p. 138). In the preschool I studied, the effects of such a shift were evident as parents questioned teachers as to why their children were not being taught to write letters and to develop graphophonemic awareness by age three. Teachers were frustrated by having parents of children ages one, two, and three ask them pointedly when their children were going to be writing their letters and reciting their alphabet, and questioning why the teachers were not employing products such as Baby Einstein™ flash-cards to accelerate their children's literacy development.

Addressing the tension I had observed in many of the classrooms, parents pushing for more structured literacy instruction and early childhood teachers feeling oppressed by such requests, I issued an invitation to teachers by e-mail as suggested by the administrator. Because the issue addressed in the invitation was real for the teachers (generated from their classrooms), many of them came to the first meeting. Yet many were skeptical because previous professional development experiences had involved detached, here-is-what-you-should-be-doing approaches. Reflecting on the experience, Lexy voiced:

> I was skeptical, but from the very beginning it was so educational and so interesting, and so just down-to-earth and personable. We were all just discussing everything, the issues we were struggling with in the classroom, our feelings, our thoughts, our teaching, and I mean I just learned SO MUCH…it was amazing to be part of a group learning together. No one knew all the answers, but just using some of the resources that they had, the ideas that they had, we just learned so much from each other.

In the first meeting, teachers showed up with notepads and pens. They slowly and quietly trickled into the room. I had reserved a space on the rug in the toddler classroom. An open space where we could sit in a circle, on the floor, to break some of the uneasiness often asso-ciated with power differentials and the traditional roles of teachers and learners. I told them that we were going to be talking about is-sues that were relevant to their own classrooms. One of the teachers (who sat right next to me) wrote "early literacy" on top of the notepad she was holding. I shared with them my experience of constraints as-sociated with literacy mandates and focused instruction. I used my own teaching experience as a codification of what they were experi-encing. Soon, the notepads and pens were put aside. Teachers began asking questions. At that point, they were still trying to find out from me what to do in their classrooms, as if I had the answer to every single question. I made it clear that I did not have all the answers and that furthermore, what worked in one classroom may not work in another classroom. I in turn posed questions and sought to listen to their experiences. They started speaking. The initial tension and skepticism was gradually transformed into a sense of curiosity. I told them that we would be meeting as often as they'd like, and that in between I would be documenting their classroom practices so the topic of our meetings would be relevant to their classroom realities.

The Teacher Educator

As a teacher educator, I wanted this professional development experience to be meaningful, so I embraced the role of an ethnographer, documenting the culture of each of the classrooms in which participants taught. Joe Kincheloe wrote that "[t]eachers working in a critical context rebel against the view of practitioners as information deliverers, as deskilled messengers who uncritically pass along a canned curriculum. Highly skilled scholarly teachers research their students and their communities" (2005, p. 108). If I was expecting teachers to engage in researching their students and the communities of which they were part, I had to embrace the same practice. I made this clear to them from the very beginning.

Over time, I collected information (e.g., audio and video recordings, field notes, artifacts) as I sought to document the cultural practices of six classrooms. As I reread the information and engaged in data reduction, I highlighted commonalities, the phenomena which were represented in situated ways across classroom contexts. Then I codified those into stories or situations or readings which would serve to get the conversation started. The process was described by one of the participating teachers, James:

> It didn't start out as open, so you didn't feel like you're walking out on a tight rope. You didn't feel like you had to bring a lot to it. At the very beginning, she would come in, and share some things we could relate to; like things that affected out classrooms, our

teaching, but not talking about us directly. Then as we started feeling comfortable, she would share different things that she would see in the classrooms from watching the videotape or observing from the booth, and then she wouldn't say where, I think, but what she saw. And by having that start off, we engaged in the discussion of a topic that was affecting our lives as teachers. Then we eventually, all the participants, became comfortable enough to, um, you know, bring your own subject matter to the table, and I think that was very smart. But what she [the facilitator] did, I think, going from talking about issues that were important to us, that were real in our classrooms, made us want to come back. When she first invited us, she got to know our classrooms. You know, if at the very beginning she'd said, oh, whatever you wanna talk about, I think that we've all, we'd all 'ave gone, um, I like kids, you know ((chuckles)), or it would become a giant gripe session, and, we'd never gone anywhere critical, we'd not seen how we have the power to change things. I think it eventually became a problem-solving session, a peer problem-solving process that valued different voices, voices from the classrooms. It was about looking at the situations we were going through and together strategizing change.

As Freire said,

> As progressive teachers and educators, we have first to get the knowledge about how the people know...we have to invent with the people the ways for them to go beyond their state of thinking...It's a starting and not a staying point (Horton & Freire, 1990, p. 98).

So, understanding the beliefs and practices of teachers was very important for me as a progressive, critical teacher educator. Not because I wanted to point fingers, but because I wanted to use that knowledge, that information as a starting point, as a way of naming the issues in order to transform them.

As a teacher educator, I saw my role as facilitating critical thinking and fostering the collective creation of a space whereby teachers could voice their thoughts, opinions, and beliefs freely and safely. According to one of the teachers, Marilyn, our teacher culture circle:

> …was a safe place for us to meet and talk about stuff. We weren't afraid of being looked down upon when we got a problem with something. It was real open. That's what I enjoyed, that's why I kept going back.

In setting up such a space and facilitating our meetings I had to walk a fine line. I was to provide focus as there were so many instances of recursive oppression being experienced by the teachers. Nevertheless, I wanted to do so in a way that would honor the teachers' choices and voices, engaging in authentic dialogue.

As a teacher educator, I started off by embracing the concept of humility. I had not taught in that setting and was not in those teachers' shoes. I had to learn alongside them and embody the premise that I was there to learn from them and with them in a true dialogic process. When I documented their practices, I earned their respect. I was not entering a professional development setting assuming that these teachers lacked certain skills or practices, I did not assume that they lacked a set of skills that I could offer. I entered this relationship on an equal basis. Authority and voice were dialogically negotiated. According to Jill, one of the participating teachers:

> Mariana [the teacher educator] was very good at bringing it back, considering many perspectives. She was good at listening, saying ok, here is what your concerns and questions are, what you discussed so far. She was just willing to steer us back to the focus of what we were doing.

I believe that over time, I negotiated and renegotiated my role as I sought to create spaces for facilitating that would not curtail the critical conversations, the dialogic exchanges, the critical process taking place. Together, we developed into a trustful community of learners and came to see the teacher culture circle as a safe yet valuable space.

Time in/and Teacher Culture Circles

One of the two biggest challenges to professional development is time; the other one is resources. In the case of teacher culture circles, it was no different. There were no resources to pay for substitutes so that teachers could meet during their regular day. We met at 5:45 pm one weekday every other week. Initially, I proposed that we meet for an hour. Eventually, our meetings developed into sessions that often lasted over two hours. Teachers would make time, after working long days, to come together. As Jill voiced:

> I would walk out of there and it was like a breath of fresh air. I just remember like, most times I'd walk out and it would be like pitch black, dark. I would be like, I haven't been home for over twelve hours, but it was like, I was fine with it because it was something that I needed. It was like a release. I feel like a lot of teachers in the professional developments I've been to before, a lot of them just wanted to gripe, and complain about a lot of things. This was different—it's just a place to breathe, it was more constructive. We could let it go, the stress, by talking about ways to change things. It was not about blaming oneself or someone else, it was about recognizing and questioning the origin of issues, being more aware, so that we could change things. We'd get feedback from each other, we work together to address issues and change things in our classroom and school.

The teacher culture circle became a treasured space for deconstructing the social construction of issues that were affecting their lives as teachers and their pedagogical practices. It was a space to confront discomfort and to question comfort. As Corry voiced:

> I always felt like I found some answers that could help me in the classroom, or that I helped somebody to find some ways to deal with and to change their situations. Through our discussions we got to the heart of issues. It was easy to say what the issues were, but our discussion took a deeper look at what was causing them, how and why they had started, if it was something contained to

our classroom, to our school, or something larger. The whole dynamic allowed us all to feel free to talk. We could say whatever we wanted to say. We were not going to be looked down on if we didn't know how to deal with a situation. That freedom to bring whatever issue to the group was empowering. Really, I think this freedom allowed us to really get to the heart of what the issues were.

While time was initially one of the main obstacles to teacher culture circles, it became one of its key components. The time in our circle allowed teachers to engage in deep conversations, in authentic dialogue (Allen, 2007), which served to problematize issues they were experiencing, and together we would strategize, problem-solve, and plan for transformative action. There was no hurrying through issues. Often our critical dialogues went on for hours and continued across meetings.

Teacher Culture Circles: The Process

The process of our teacher culture circle developed over time. As situations changed, topics changed accordingly. But also, as teachers became more familiar and comfortable with the process, they took ownership and made decisions to extend or re-envision some of the traditional components of Freirean culture circles. For example, at times, instead of stopping with action, teachers reported back to the group on the consequences of their actions. This often meant going back through the transformative critical cycle once more, to address remaining complexities. At other times, this practice provided the encouragement needed for another teacher to promote change in his/her own setting.

Sitting in a Circle

Trying to respect the teachers' preferences, I asked them where they'd like to meet. While I was adamant that we had to sit in a circle for pedagogical reasons, I was open to meeting in a location of their choice. The teachers chose to meet in a classroom in the preschool where they taught. Every other week at 5:30 pm on the appointed day, I made my way there. I would make sure that the rug area where we met was ready and I would wait for them.

Nevertheless, the role of the facilitator goes beyond setting the physical space. According to Bahruth and Steiner (2000):

> Orchestrating a culture circle is intellectually demanding and requires constant reflection and criticity of one's own pedagogy. The physical space is arranged in an attempt to provide pedagogical spaces in which students can develop their voices in a human environment of respect and affirmation. Arranging students in a circle is a pedagogical move whereby the physical environment of the classroom is transformed from the straight row, front-facing arrangements found in traditional classrooms. The change in physical arrangements provides the opportunity for a change in the human environment in the classroom as well; however, other changes must accompany this arrangement if a culture circle is to evolve...To complete the shift the teacher must also consider a change in discourse patterns and views of authority, knowledge, curriculum, and learning. What is apparent is that a culture circle does not evolve simply by having students sit in a circle. (p. 122)

Beyond setting up the physical space to challenge traditionally conceived classrooms where adult learning takes place (e.g., rows of desks), I wanted to provide a space that would break the traditional power hierarchy of standard professional development sessions. So, as opposed to asking teachers to come to an unfamiliar space, we met in a very familiar space for all of them—a classroom in the preschool. They all felt comfortable there.

Generative Themes: Where It All Begins

As explained in Chapter 2, generative themes unfold from lived experiences. In applying culture circles to in-service teacher education, I initially documented the important and recurring issues present in the lives of these teachers and codified them, bringing them to the group to be discursively deconstructed, decoded, problematized. Eventually, participating teachers started providing their own experiences, presented as codified stories, vignettes, or problems.

In culture circles, participating teachers are protagonists in the professional development, as the process is centered around their lives and experiences. Initially, generative themes are codified into stories, video clips, pictures, etc. Codification is the representation of a meaningful aspect of the teacher's experience. The benefit of this representation is that it allows teachers to analyze a situation from a non-threatening theoretical viewpoint while still making connections with the situation of their own practices.

So, prior to conducting the professional development, those organizing and conducting professional development within a culture circle must learn from the schools/classrooms and teachers' practices. Conducting ethnographic research, they observe and record common situations in that particular context. Those themes relevant to the teachers become the core of the professional development opportunity. These lists are then codified into stories, pictures or other visual representations. Consequently, teachers are able to engage in deeper dialogue, as the method focuses on their strengths, on their knowledge regarding those words and themes that emerged from their own universe, as opposed to accentuating the areas in which their practices might need further honing.

From Accepting to Challenging

As we got started, my challenge was to help teachers identify conscious and unconscious ways in which they attempted to derail the dialogue. Because so many of them had been socialized into accepting what they were told as opposed to questioning, problematizing, challenging and changing, in the beginning they attempted to halt critical dialogue by saying "it's just the way it is," "we have to do it," and other similar statements. I facilitated further dialogue by making teachers aware of the social construction of oppressive situations. The main way I did so was by asking follow-up questions, seeking to uncover the complex, multi-layered nature of oppressions. The dialogue below represents one such attempt:

Lexy: But we have to do it. It doesn't matter if it's not the best for the kids. Now we cannot have water play anymore.

Mariana: Why?

Lexy: Because of accreditation.

Mariana: Tell me more. You mean, accreditation will make things worse for the kids?

Corry: Yes, because now we cannot have water play outside because we have to change the water every time that a child plays with water.

Mariana: But, do you have to meet every single standard to meet accreditation?

Marilyn: I don't know.

Shante: No. Only a percentage.

Mariana: So, can you use their system to your advantage?

Marilyn: I guess we are teachers, we are so accustomed to playing by the rules, you know.

Mariana: Who makes the rules?

Hillary: NAEYC.

Mariana: NAEYC?

Hillary: Yeah, the organization that accredits preschools.

Mariana: But who at NAEYC made those decisions?

Shante: I don't know, some people I guess.

Lexy: Some people who might not know how impossible it is to change the water [in the water table] after each child or group of children play.

Mariana: So, what if they made a rule you didn't agree with? Would you play by the rules if the rule was to exclude children with disabilities?

Lexy: No way.

Mariana: So, when do you follow the rules?

Hillary: When they are fair.

Shante: Aren't all rules fair?

Mariana: Are they?

James: No, no, no, no.

Mariana: So, what can we do?

Lexy: I guess we can work together to choose what is important and what we are not willing to change.

James: Right.

Marilyn: And we can work together, so we have the power to say that we don't agree with it.

These teachers were accustomed to following the rules passed down from administrators. By asking follow-up questions, I sought to uncover ways to find wiggle room within the system, to engage in advocacy for child-centered practices. Taking a critical stance meant problematizing issues instead of accepting them, asking questions and seeking to change unfair practices.

As a facilitator, I was not attempting to lead them "to a singular destination other than the evolution of their criticity" (Bahruth & Steiner, 2000, p. 123). I wanted them to be critical, to pose problems and not to accept everything just because it already existed. By engaging in critical dialogue, I wanted to push them beyond what *is* to what *could be*.

While I did ask questions, I did not know where the circle was going and what twists and turns may be presented by the teachers' perspectives and voices. For example, when Marilyn said "I guess we are teachers, we are so accustomed to playing by the rules, you know," I could have accepted her explanation, but instead I posed more issues and tried to get them to consider the fairness of rules and the fact that rules were created by human beings. I did not have an expectation regarding the direction of the conversation. If I had an expectation, a mental script of how the dialogue would happen, I would be negating the critical nature of circles.

As a critical teacher educator, I wanted participating teachers to question, to problematize, to start seeing spaces of possibility and to persistently engage in posing problems to change their practices—in their classrooms and in their worlds. I agree with Genishi and Dyson (2009) that "through educators' persistent, child-worthy efforts in classrooms and the larger public arena, we can look toward a future where children and teachers can work and play with less pressure and greater flexibility" (p. 145).

Teachers make decisions based on their life experiences. If they were accustomed to following rules, for example, they would likely continue following rules, perhaps even without questioning the fairness of such rules. According to Bahruth and Steiner (2000), "Rather than dismissing their life experiences, the teacher recognizes that students can only make new meanings based upon prior understandings anchored in the organic nature of their knowing" (p. 123). Critical teacher education begins "by deconstructing prior school experiences in the mainstream" (p. 123).

Through this teacher culture circle, I was able to act upon the belief that "...practicing teachers need to gain a more complex conceptual understanding of the multiple contexts in which education takes place and the plethora of forces shaping the process" (Kincheloe, 2005, p. 101). In a small way, I was able to help teachers engage in more critical thought processes, whereby they engaged in problematizing and challenging issues as opposed to accepting everything as fixed and unchangeable constructs and realities.

Problem Posing

In a critical culture circle, participants pose problems as they try to understand a situation. In this particular culture circle, teachers questioned practices that were taken for granted within their professional contexts, becoming more critically aware of the origin and meaning of the values they called their own and how they compared to developmentally appropriate practices (Bredekamp & Copple, 2009). In doing so, they asked questions such as: "Why do you think this is happening?" "Who could help you with this?" "But...how did it get started?" "How does it affect classroom dynamics?" "Is this developmentally appropriate?" As they problematized the situation presented (codified representations of a common event that was occurring in the teachers' classrooms), they started dialoguing and listening to each other. According to the teachers in our culture circle, this happened because "they can relate to what's going on."

Freire (1997) used problem posing to initiate dialogue. This is exactly what I did here for transformative professional development. Instead of providing solutions, I asked questions, I raised issues and challenged the status quo. Such problem posing led to dialogue. Taking the teachers' experiences as central to the professional development process respects their practices while at the same time makes learning memorable and relevant to their contexts. This was important as knowledge is not only historical, epistemological, and logical, but it is dialogical (Gadotti, 1994). Through dialogue, we open the doors to rethinking our practices and transforming our classrooms. Hence, problem-posing participants' experiences is key to this kind of professional development.

Dialogically Offering Perspectives and Problem Solving

According to one of the participating teachers, one of the more powerful aspects of our teacher culture circle was that there were different, and at times conflicting, views being exposed. Jill said with regard to the teacher culture circle:

> It was a safe place, and I found very quickly that all of us were very DIFFERENT. I mean we were all working toward the same goal, but we're doing it in different ways, we have different personalities, and that difference just brought a lot to the group. There were many instances when either we might disagree or we might talk about subjects that might be a little uncomfortable for a lot of people because we have different belief systems and different experiences. Mostly, things started uncomfortable. Identifying problems is not something we group up doing and being praised for doing it. But it got better as we saw ways to change things. And that difference helped us consider many ways of changing the situations, the issues. For example, when we exposed a situation, it was uncomfortable, but as we talked and listened to each other, considered many solutions, we felt more

comfortable—not comfortable with the situation, but capable of our ability to change it. Sometimes, we could not address an issue in one meeting and left with it unsettled. It DIDN'T happen that often.

According to Victoria Purcell-Gates and Robin Waterman (2000), the "alternative to banking is dialogue and critique" (p. 12). As a teacher educator seeking to do away with the transfer of decontextualized knowledges, ready answers and solutions for classrooms, I wanted to foster critical dialogue. Together with the teachers, I engaged in critical thinking and sought to develop critical meta-awareness by considering the larger issues and discourses shaping the situated representations of phenomena which were affecting many teachers within the preschool and across classrooms (Dyson & Genishi, 2005). We sought to engage in a critical understanding of our situations and locations, considering sociocultural and historical inequities that had over time shaped the world we knew. Together, we sought to "alter these situations toward creating a more just and equal social and political world" (Purcell-Gates & Waterman, 2000, p. 12). In our teacher culture circles, dialogue helped us move in that direction. We blurred the role of teacher and teacher educator (Freire, 1970), as we were all dynamically and simultaneously positioned as teachers and learners. Together, we challenged teacher education as transmission of knowledge and redefined it as the creation and recreation of knowledge through authentic, egalitarian, and critical dialogue.

James recounted:

It was an open, a safe space. I remember going to a meeting and another teacher saying, I've got to talk about this right now. As we realized we were facing similar issues, we just sat down and laid the problem out. We just talked about it. We didn't know the answers. We all had questions. Each of us kind of took a little bit of it and talked about part; why do you see this happening, what might be causing it, how is it similar or different across contexts? Then we'd go, maybe if you try this. I think it was beneficial for us as teachers, to dialogue, to peer problem-solve. Alone, we were in hermetically sealed bubbles, but together we could change the world.

Through critical dialogue, we began to read our worlds and words continuously, recursively, and collectively. As individuals, we came together and developed an awareness of the collective nature of issues, forming a community of learners that engaged in deconstructing layers of social-political meanings and challenging institutional discourses. Collectively and dialogically, we came to see ourselves as historical beings, as teachers located within sociocultural and historical contexts and occupying political spaces. We came to see ourselves for our collective power to embrace and co-create transformation.

Dialogue and Problem Solving

"Problem-solving dialogue begins with questions...This practical method of frontloading student discourse is what Freire would call a "praxis" of dialogue and what Dewey would call an "agency" of democratic education—that is, practical means to put theory into action" (Shor, 1996, p. 41). Teacher educators and those conducting professional development must know and believe that dialogue is the essential condition of our work—our job is to coordinate and to facilitate, but never to impose. When there is imposition, there is also greater resistance.

In a dialogue with Paulo Freire (Shor & Freire, 1987), Ira Shor said:

> I like the irony of consciousness that makes liberation possible. By studying our lack of freedom we can learn how to become free. This is the dialectic of the liberatory class. It's one place where we think critically about the forces interfering with our critical thought. So, liberatory classes illuminate the conditions we're in to help overcome those conditions, offering students a critical distance on society in place of an uncritical immersion in the status quo, to think of changing it. (p. 14)

The aim of critical dialogue is conscientization of each participant's context, population, and condition. According to Darder (2002), dialogue is the foundation of critical pedagogy. Thus critical problem posing happens dialogically. For example, in one professional development session, I observed a teacher who, contrary to popular belief, claimed that choice was inappropriate for every child, that it created chaos and disorganization in her classroom. She was concerned and felt that she was failing. After she posed her problem, the group discussed it and came up with suggestions to address the situation. The group concluded that it was necessary to expose children to the available activities, to share known ways to engage in choice activities, and to create new ways to engage with the available choices. Furthermore, the group suggested that perhaps the children could negotiate, co-construct new activities altogether.

Changing Agency

As I engaged in coding data from the teacher culture circle, I identified representative phenomena. I employed *Critical Narrative Analysis* (Souto-Manning, 2005) to analyze words and worlds (Freire, 1970), and shared the process with participating teachers. To do so, I combine Critical Discourse Analysis (Fairclough, 2003) and Conversational Narrative Analysis (Ochs & Capps, 2001), establishing Critical Narrative Analysis to reach a more complete analysis. Narrative Analysis examines how people make sense of their experiences in society through language (Ochs & Capps, 2001). Critical Discourse Analysis involves power and language within the context of society (Fairclough, 2003). Critical Narrative Analysis, CNA (Souto-Manning, 2005) aims at promoting meta-awareness, *conscientização* (Freire, 1970), allowing people to engage in social action to solve problems and address issues identified in their narratives.

Critical Narrative Analysis mirrors the process whereby teachers engage in questioning their generative stories and locations in society. CNA emerged from my study of the Freirean critical cycle itself

(Souto-Manning, 2005; 2007) and, as such, is an integral part of what goes on in three of the components of culture circles—problem posing, dialogue, and problem solving. Through generative stories (situated representation of themes), teachers began collectively questioning their realities and problem solving; after all, storytelling is a site for problem solving (Ochs, Smith & Taylor, 1996). Teachers then came to recognize institutional discourses recycled within their narratives (intertextually), challenged them and ultimately engaged in action.

The teachers' conversational narratives at first conveyed the morality to which they oriented (the right thing to do) based on generic ideas of "best practice" and "developmentally appropriate practice" (DAP) without regard for culturally specific/relevant practices and bodies of knowledge. After joining culture circle study groups, they constructed a situated, collective moral compass, developing a sense of collective agency, cultural awareness and responsiveness. As their narratives changed, they gained a sense of agency through personal action and shifting internal conversations. I found that their narratives aligned with the goal of social action and change proposed by culture circles.

As teachers started redrafting stories, they shifted reflexivities and narratives. In terms of reflexivities, they started appropriating language and questioning status quo. This was confirmed by actions such as the implementation of culturally responsive practices in their classrooms even when such practices conflicted with developmentally appropriate practices. For example, teachers found that while DAP promoted independence in terms of infants and toddlers self-feeding, in many homes and cultural contexts which valued interdependence over independence (Souto-Manning, 2009c), self-feeding at an early age was not a desirable behavior for some children according to their familial and cultural practices.

In terms of narratives, change was signaled by framing agency and grammatical agency (Souto-Manning, 2005). Teachers started seeing themselves as capable of promoting change. In terms of grammatical agency, they went from "**I wasn't given** an opportunity to learn and grow as a teacher" to "**We decide** the important things for us to discuss and work on together," thereby positioning themselves as subjects who commit actions and promote change. In terms of framing agency (how they morally positioned themselves and their actions), they went from "**I couldn't** build on what the children brought to the classroom. I had to focus on the curriculum and not on the child" (framing self according to DAP morals) to "Now I want to honor every student's background and build on their strengths. **I can do this** and I know other teachers are ready to pitch in and work together to make this happen" (framing self according to a collective moral compass). Consequently, agency was developing as indicated by their texts and contexts.

Furthermore, participating teachers moved towards agency as indicated by the turning points in their narratives. For example, in the narrative below, Shante indicated that her turning point came in the teacher culture circle, signaling the power of culture circles in influencing teachers' practices and beliefs.

> Shante: I thought, okay, I can't do anything here. Something needs to change, but I can't be the one responsible, you know. Maybe I'll leave. But then...

TURNING POINT

...I, we became part of the teacher study group. It was wonderful. I had a renewed sense of purpose...We knew that we could change anything if we stuck together. We learned that we didn't need to know everything. That we could learn along the way. If I needed help, if anyone needed help, we were there for each other.

Towards Action

According to Celia Genishi and Anne Haas Dyson (2009), "Advocacy is possible when people join language together with action—when they develop socially and politically focused "language-and-action" ways" (p. 145). Together in culture circles, the teachers developed language-and-action ways to transform their situations and change their locations. They became advocates for the children they educated and for each other. They came to recognize themselves as change agents.

As teachers problem-solved dialogically, they moved towards collectively envisioning spaces for transformation and engaged in planning ways to carry out their plans. After carrying out their planned course of action, teachers (individually and/or collectively) reported back to the group. As mentioned earlier, this extra step, coming back to dialogically reflect on action, sometimes meant beginning the cycle again as new issues were uncovered and needed to be problematized. When this was the case, the group repeated the critical cycle process. If all went well and the action worked as planned or addressed the issue at hand, teachers got to celebrate with fellow participants. This extra step extended Freire's method, strengthening and unifying the community of learners. As a result, teachers felt confident about their abilities to promote change in their classrooms.

Learnings

In implementing this approach, I learned that early childhood educators found this professional development model engaging and relevant. As I employed this kind of professional development with early childhood educators, they voiced comments such as "I can't wait to try this in my classroom" and "This is so helpful." I share this approach with you here in hopes that it will be helpful and inspire you to engage in reflective practice in your school and/or classroom.

There were direct benefits for the preschool. All teachers who participated in the teacher culture circle furthered their education by subsequently pursuing advanced degrees. Many teachers developed as action researchers and engaged in collaborative research projects. Some of the teachers are employing culture circle pedagogy in their own early childhood classrooms. Finally, there was a lower teacher attrition rate at the school where they worked (from 30% to under 10%) following the implementation of in-service teacher culture circles. While there are many factors which might have influenced these outcomes, the participating teachers themselves indicated that they observed direct links between the teacher culture circle and these particular results.

A year after I stopped facilitating the teacher study group, the teachers petitioned upper administrators at the university where the preschool was located to create a structure whereby they could continue having their own space to discuss issues. Furthermore, together they requested a liaison who would represent the teacher culture circle and serve as a bridge between teachers and administrators, seeking to negotiate action. In devising such a process, the teachers used the power of their collectiveness to become more active and present in the decision-making processes that shaped the everyday life of the preschool. By doing so, they engaged in the positive institutionalization of the critical cycle.

Inspired by their collective action, I conclude this chapter with an invitation to embrace the critical cycle of questioning and problem posing. I hope that you inquire, as educators and teacher educators, "What are we rethinking? What are we doing to advocate social justice? And what could we be doing differently?" (Genishi & Goodwin, 2008, p. 273). In considering these questions and dialoguing about them with a community of learners, I hope you will see the paramount role of culture circles in moving the field forward through engagement in critical and transformative pedagogical action.

CHAPTER 7

Performing Culture Circles: Boalian Theatre in Teacher Education

Theater is change and not simple presentation of what exists: it is becoming and not being.

Boal (2000, p. 28)

T*heatre of the Oppressed* (T.O.) was established by Brazilian theatre director and Workers' Party (PT) political activist Augusto Boal (1931-2009). Boal was director of the Teatro Arena group from 1958 to 1970, during which time he developed what is now known as the Theatre of the Oppressed (Silva, 2009). He was inspired by the ideas of Paulo Freire's landmark treatise in education, *Pedagogy of the Oppressed* (1970). There is no clear explanation as to how or when Boal and Freire met, yet Freire's ideas deeply influenced Boal's work. He was a friend and colleague of Paulo Freire. Boal (2005) recounted:

Paulo Freire was a very good friend of mine, and he started more or less in the 1960s. Once we were talking to try to remember when we have met for the first time. We do not remember well. We had the impression that we have met for all our lives. And his work inspired me, of course, and did develop parallel one to another. But of course he wrote the *Pedagogy of the Oppressed* first, and by title Theater of the Oppressed is a homage to him. (¶ 13)

Because of their strong connection, Augusto Boal referred to Paulo Freire as his "last father" when Freire passed away on May 2, 1997. Coincidentally, Boal passed away 12 years after Freire on May 2, 2009.

It is easy to notice how Freire's theory permeated Boal's practice in *Theatre of the Oppressed*, a performative version of the concepts presented in *Pedagogy of the Oppressed*. Both of them forefronted the codification of themes and narratives by focusing on generative themes and situations, and sought to problematize everyday realities that were oppressive and helped maintain the imbalanced social status quo by which the rich and powerful oppressed the lower class. The work of Brazilian theatre activist Augusto Boal was one of the first approaches to conceptualize the intersections of art, drama therapy, and social revolution.

Born in Rio de Janeiro and formally trained as an engineer, Boal's work contributed much to the demechanization of the human body and the challenging of social stereotypes and psychological assumptions through theatre. While experimenting with non-traditional theatre methods in São Paulo, Brazil, Boal developed a more engaged and interactive form of theatre. Instead of an audience reacting to plays only after they ended, in the 1960s Boal conceptualized the spectator as an active participant in theatrics. Instead of waiting for the curtains to draw in order to articulate their thoughts and reactions verbally, Boal invited spectators to become "spect-actors," a hybrid of spectator and actor.

Under Boal's direction spect-actors had the power to interrupt the acting and offer alternative actions to the character being oppressed. Initially this occurred in a more verbal way as audience members would propose actions to be performed by the professional actor playing the character/role. Later on, the true meaning of spect-actor came to life as a woman, frustrated that the actor could not understand her verbal suggestions, stepped onto the stage and replaced the oppressed character herself.

Spect-actors became a common part of Boal's experiments, as those suggesting alternative courses of action were invited to step up and replace the actor, playing the role of the oppressed a different way. Participants had the power to change the situations directly through demonstration and performance. When performing the suggested change, actors came to feel empowered and started conceptualizing themselves as agents—as subjects who can act upon and change oppressive situations, rather than as objects, victims of other people's actions. They began rehearsing the revolution. By reflectively dialoguing about the suggested courses of action, participants collectively became empowered and sought to engage in social action. Theatre of the Oppressed became a tool, a medium for activism.

Originally T.O. was designed for working with peasants in Brazil. As it became a method for rehearsing and carrying out changes, it was seen as a threat. Cultural activist Boal was declared dangerous to the military government. After the coup d'etat of 1964, in which the military overtook the Brazilian government accusing the elected president of being communist, Both Paulo Freire and Augusto Boal were sent to other Latin American countries. Boal was kidnapped in 1971 as he returned home from the performance of a play he directed. First exiled to Argentina and then to Peru, he later went to Europe.

During his exile, as Freire had also done, Boal wrote his landmark work concerning social oppression—*Teatro del Oprimido* (1974). This book was subsequently translated into *Theatre of the Oppressed* (1979) a few years after the 1970 publication of *Pedagogy of the Oppressed* by Paulo Freire. About ten years after his exile, during which he continued to teach his liberatory activist theatre throughout the world, Boal orchestrated the first International Festival of the Theatre of the Oppressed in Paris (Paterson, 2005). Following the fall of the military government in Brazil, Boal returned to Rio de Janeiro in the mid-1980s.

After democracy returned to Brazil, a popular movement developed named *Diretas Já!* (trans. Direct [elections] now!) in which people went to the streets protesting for direct elections. In the mid-

eighties elections took place and Boal, back in his native Rio de Janeiro, was elected to the office of *vereador* (a full-time, fully-funded
city council–like position), and established venues for teaching and
performing his theatre. Despite his failed re-election campaign, he
continued using forms of T.O. to raise awareness of local issues in
neighborhoods and communities throughout Rio de Janeiro.

In the U.S. and Canada "Theatre of the Oppressed" has been
called different names, such as "Theatre of Liberation," "Theatre for
Living," and "Redo Theatre." Augusto Boal's methods were first
explicitly linked to higher education in the United States in 1992,
when he was a keynote speaker for the National Conference of the
Association of Theatre in Higher Education. This was the year in
which Boal's *Games for Actors and Non-Actors* was published (first in
French, then translated to English), and became a must-read for those
already using T.O. It also provided a thorough and theoretically
sound introduction for those new to T.O., the non-actors. It defined
theatre that is not only enjoyable, but educational and revolutionary
as well. *Games for Actors and Non-Actors* couched theatre as social
therapy that presented people with new perspectives on old,
oppressive, and recurring situations. It also provided exercises for
demechanizing the body, for challenging habits our muscles are
familiar with, challenging the physical status quo. It presented
methods, techniques, games, and exercises that easily come to life,
that are simple to use.

Key Components and Practices

Boalian Theatre is an umbrella term that encompasses practices such
as games for actors and various performance models. As Freirean
pedagogy was

> ...motivated by a genuine desire for dialogue—a belief that in this process the
> "students" have knowledge which the "teacher" needs to learn. This was the
> approach Boal adopted. Just as Freire had outlined the methods whereby
> students within the educational process could make the transition from seeing
> themselves as objects (unconscious and acted upon by others) to subjects
> (capable of self-conscious action) Boal identified stages by which the spectator—

in his view fundamentally a passive being—would become an actor. The proposed steps are as follows: (1) knowing the body; (2) making the body expressive; (3) theatre as language; and (4) the theatre as discourse. (Babbage, 2004, p. 20)

From his work Boal evolved various forms of theatre and performance which aim to meet the needs of all people through interaction, dialogue, critical thinking, action, and fun. While the performance modes of Forum Theatre, Image Theatre, Cop-In-The-Head, Rainbow of Desire, Invisible Theatre and Legislative Theatre are designed to bring the audience into active relationship with the performed event, the Games for Actors and Non-Actors are virtually a training ground for action not only in these performance forms, but for action in life.

Boal's workshops focused on ways that participants could apply T.O. to their own contexts, and make a difference in their own locations. He began his workshops with theatre games for actors and non-actors. Such games were designed to engage the body in dynamism, moving away from our habitual movements. The movements we habitually perform imprison us and result in us becoming physically incapable of exploring physical and social imagination. *So cool!*

Key Roles

Key roles in Boalian *Theatre of the Oppressed* are those of the **Spect-Actor** and **Joker**. Below, I explore the complexities and multidimensionalities of such roles and parallel them with the dynamic and interchangeable roles of teacher/facilitator and learner essential to the critical cycle of Freire's *Pedagogy of the Oppressed*.

Spect-Actors

Boal created the term spect-actor to break the division between stage and audience and engage all participants equally in generating the plot of the story between Antagonist and Protagonist. Spect-actors offer different solutions the Protagonist might take by actually getting on stage and performing the suggested alternative thereby blurring the lines and roles of subject and object, teacher and learner, actor and spectator.

Joker: Facilitator or "Difficultator"?

Much of Augusto Boal's theatrical process requires a neutral party at the center of proceedings. This person takes responsibility for the logistical running of the process and ensures a fair proceeding. In Freirean culture circles, the role of this individual is fulfilled by the *Facilitator*. In Boal's literature this role is often referred to as the *Joker* in reference to the neutrality of the Joker card in a deck of playing cards.

Some of the roles of the Joker, the facilitator, or the "difficultator" (as Boal preferred to identify the role) include generating participation, stimulating reluctant audiences, to "difficultate" interventions, working with particular constituencies, and knowing how and when to end a show. Boal played the role of the "Joker," a role that is simultaneously director, facilitator, and critic, asking the spect-actors the question: is it real? Is the solution presented by the spect-actors possible? If not, then the group would collectively decide to rehearse other possibilities for the future, or, as Boal would say, "to rehearse for the revolution."

Why Theatre?
Exploring Possibilities in Teacher Education

Why theatre? "Because performance itself is grounded in action, reflexivity, and dialogue, a critical performative pedagogy denies students the comfort of a quiet, object position" (Louis, 2005, p. 344). Because theatre is more than actor training; it is human training, a site to learn the possibilities of being human (Boal, 2000). Because theatre opens up a space for critical performative pedagogy and embraces a language of possibility as participants engage performatively in contexts, possibilities and realities.

Performance can be a mode for opening up an array of possibilities and perspectives which move individuals away from oppression. "[P]erformativity helps to locate and describe repetitive patterns plotted within grids of power relationships and social norms within the context of education" (Alexander, Anderson, & Gallegos, 2005, p. 2). It creates a "liminal space capable of disrupting the social order" and committed to using performance as a tool in "human training." (Louis, 2005, p. 337). Performance can serve as agency, since through performance, participants occupy both the location of body and subject; agents capable of promoting change in society (Boal, 2000). According to Howard (2004), Boalian theatre can serve as a bridge between critical theory and classroom practice, as it offers an "alternative language to discuss, analyze, and resolve oppressions" (p. 220). Boal proposed that such language needs to be "placed at the service of the oppressed" (1974, p. 22).

In teacher education, concern has been expressed that multiculturalism is too often entirely text-based, whereby students read and feel a cathartic release, experiencing the oppression through text and leaving the classroom without any real social engagement. The discourse in most teacher education classrooms is one of monologue in which the teacher delivers knowledge and participants are reduced to silence and obedience. Theatre of the Oppressed has been used to counter traditional forms of education oriented toward single-answer solutions, and it can act as a framework for critical performance and change in teacher education.

T.O. in multicultural teacher education encourages problem posing rather than finite solutions and can therefore alter teacher education in significant ways. Teacher education must "consider the ways in which a given site's subject matter gets altered by a critical, embodied pedagogy, taking into account students' material uses for that subject matter and the means by which social critique and action enter the site" (Louis, 2005, p. 348). The context for learning becomes one of embodied sites of practice where education is transitive—that is, the experiences of teacher participants inform and influence teacher educators and vice versa. The collective practice of T.O. becomes a rehearsal for real social action in teachers' lives. And the teacher education classroom is transformed into a dialogue for collective engagement rather than a monologue for a grade.

Monologues are locations/situations/oppressive conditions in which only one interlocutor has the right to speak. In teacher education this interlocutor is typically the teacher educator. Freire conceived turning monologue into dialogue, turning banking education into dialogic conversations that are transitive, in which each participant is an influence on the other in true interactive dialogue as opposed to serial monologue.

Furthermore, instead of embracing a banking approach to teacher education in which knowledge is deposited in students' brains as money in banks (Freire, 1970), Theatre of the Oppressed allows relationships of power and conflict to be explored. One of the most powerful aspects of Boalian Theatre is the possibility it presents for crossing time and space boundaries. In Theatre of the Oppressed workshops, teacher educators embrace and expand their commitment to rehearsing change and to promoting social justice even when teachers are not ordinarily geographically close. Teachers come to one workshop and by stepping into a situation deemed relevant by the group, experience many of the interactional and contextual issues shaping the situation, therefore having a realistic experience without leaving the teacher education classroom. A situated representation follows.

Why Boalian Theatre in
Early Childhood Teacher Education?[4]

Research studies have suggested a high rate of teacher burnout and stress particular to early childhood education (Manlove, 1994; Warnemuende, 1996). According to Pineau (2002), traditional teacher

---

[4] An earlier version of this and subsequent sections of this chapter were published in: Souto-Manning, M., Cahnmann-Taylor, M., Dice, J., & Wooten, J. (2008). The power and possibilities of performative critical early childhood teacher education. *Journal of Early Childhood Teacher Education*, 29 (4), 309-325.

education relies on problem and solution posing through discussion and does not explore other ways of opening up opportunities for social action.

In Souto-Manning, Cahnmann-Taylor, Dice, & Wooten (2008), we proposed that critical performance can be a mode for opening up an array of possibilities and perspectives which move new teachers away from thinking and feeling they are powerless toward changing limiting conditions in their professional lives. A performative model of early childhood teacher education has the potential to help with the identification of patterns of interaction situated within relationships laden with power differentials and bound by social norms (Alexander, Anderson, & Gallegos, 2005). By making discursive and behavior patterns a point of rehearsal and revision, performance can promote agency and lead to transformation at the personal and/or societal levels.

Based on Paulo Freire's *Pedagogy of the Oppressed* (1970), and aimed at challenging and transforming oppressive situations through praxis, Boalian Theatre can bridge critical theory with classroom practice as it offers an alternative platform for examining underlying assumptions in social interaction (Howard, 2004). Theatre of the Oppressed can serve as a tool to counter traditional forms of education oriented toward single-answer solutions, and teacher as isolated individual. As exemplified in the case study presented in this chapter, T.O. may serve as a framework for critical performance, sensitivity to diversity, and positive change in teacher education.

By encouraging problem posing rather than finite solutions, and dialogue rather than monologue, Theatre of the Oppressed can alter early childhood teacher education in a significant way. After all, there is no single and simple solution to conflicts, but a gamut of perspectives and possible solutions which are based on interactional contexts. "[T]he ways that people interact...depend on context—the frameworks for interpretation—that people bring to those experiences...Context is itself a complex concept, whose meaning is not fixed" (Dyson & Genishi, 2005, p. 5). The context for learning moves toward embodied sites of practice where education is transitive—that is, the experiences of teacher participants inform and influence teacher educators and vice versa. The collective practice of Theatre of the Oppressed becomes a rehearsal for real social action in teachers' lives, especially in the context of the early childhood classroom where educators are often in constant collaboration with other adult educators. In addition, it is developmentally and culturally appropriate as it uses teachers' experiences as points of departure.

Relationships, Power, and Conflict in the Early Childhood Classroom

In early childhood education, lead and assistant teachers usually work together to meet teacher-student ratios recommended by the National Association for the Education of Young Children (NAEYC) and/or by licensing bodies in a financially savvy way—it is cheaper to pay an assistant teacher than to pay an additional lead teacher to lower ratios. Usually, an assistant teacher is assigned to a lead teacher by administrators, and the teacher must figure out how to navigate their relationship and deal with conflict. Borrowing from the literature on family functioning, two caregivers who are in conflict may be less emotionally available and have an adverse impact on how children act and react (Katz & Woodin, 2002; Sturge-Apple, Davies, & Cummings, 2006). In the case of a classroom with lead and assistant teachers in conflict, there is likely less emotional availability for the children. It is best for the children if their teachers (whether lead or assistant) can work towards finding viable solutions to conflicts and oppression. As young children learn what they live, those underlying conflicts (whether overt of covert) can permeate children's interactions and hinder their development (Tegano, Groves, & Catron, 1999). Therefore, knowing how to deal with conflict while respecting perspectives is beneficial to early educators as well as to the children they serve.

New turns in critical scholarship view conflict as dynamic, unpredictable, and filled with potential for change. Cowhey (2006) discussed the importance of embracing conflict to encourage critical and diverse thinking. In the critical performative approach presented here, multiple solutions are presented collectively by spect-actors, leading to respect for other people's views and perspectives. Such a process is represented by Figure 7.1 (below) which builds upon and parallels the critical cycle presented in Part I (see Figure 1.1). By engaging in this process and embracing a multitude of possible solutions and perspectives, teachers can better engage in diversity teaching as they see their own stances as culturally-situated (Rogoff, 2003).

Critical Performative Early Childhood Teacher Education

The critical cycle inherent to Freirean culture circles includes generative themes, problematization, dialogue, problem solving, and action. This cycle is illustrated in Part I (Chapters 1 and 2), and parallel to the Boalian critical performative process which is also cyclical and recursive, presenting the five phases outlined in Figure 7.1 below.

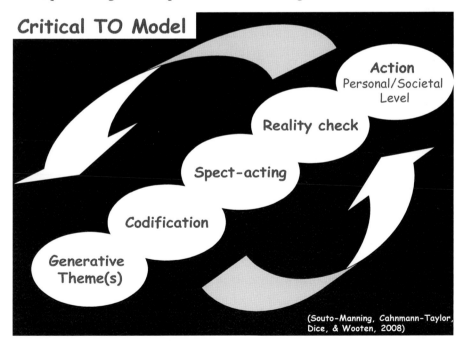

Figure 7.1: A critical performative model of early childhood teacher education.

1. **Generative Theme(s)**: The texts employed in the critical class-room are generated from participants' lives, narratives and experiences (Freire, 1970). These experiences represent situations in which they experienced recurring oppression.

2. **Codification**: Teachers codify their experiences as they select a relevant situation by scripting their narratives into a three-scene enactment portraying the oppressed person (Protagonist) and the person serving in the role of oppressor (Antagonist).

3. **Spect-acting**: As the Antagonist and Protagonist enact the scene, spect-actors can stop the action at anytime, replace one of the actors and improvise a new (re)action, which is then interactionally validated or challenged.

4. **Reality Check**: As multiple instances of spect-acting occur, there are opportunities for reality checks which may clarify the situation, taking into consideration the temperament and identity of the Protagonist.

5. **Action**: In this last phase, there is collective and individual plotting of action, both on the individual and on the societal levels.

This process, similar to culture circles, but performative and physical rather than verbal and dialogic, may not be as linear as portrayed by Figure 7.1 as there is much back and forth negotiation among phases which do not present finite boundaries.

Theatre of the Oppressed differs from role playing as it is open ended and there is no definitive solution, but rather a multitude of possibilities. The key is to problem pose, rather than problem solve at the onset. Edmond and Tilley (2007) explored how theatre goes beyond role playing as it more fully explores contexts and interactional nuances. Theatre of the Oppressed goes beyond simple theatre as it allows for the possibility of rendering multiple performances (and therefore behaviors) of the same episode (which is generated from participating teachers' experiences). The process works in the following manner:

1. Participants share their narratized struggles with the collective (generative themes).
2. The collective dialogically decides on a narrative that is representative of some of the oppressions they experience in their own particular contexts and the selected narrative is broken into three scenes by the collective (codification).
3. The sequence of three scenes is acted for the first time. At any time during the rendering of the situation, any of the participants can trade places, acting simultaneously as both spectators and actors (spect-actors). Possible solutions and/or perspectives are presented through acting, as spectators trade places with actors. Several reenactments ensue, exactly how many depends on the time available. Per our experience, spect-actors can come up with multiple solutions and we have not experienced any instances in which spect-actors ran out of solutions before two or three hours had elapsed. The process is cyclical and recurring (spect-acting).
4. As different solutions are presented, the author of the narrative is given the right of refusal by executing a reality check and answering whether that specific suggestion could be real and applicable to the particular context (reality check).
5. After the session, teachers take perspectives and possible solutions that they deem real and apply them to their particular contexts (action).

According to interview data, this process is helpful not only to the particular person who shared the situation, but to others as well, as they employ it as a tool to deal with conflict and oppression. As a result of this process, we have seen instances of change at the personal level (e.g., "I can deal with this," "I feel so much better") and at the contextual level (e.g., "I changed schools," "I talked to the principal"). While change is not always immediate, according to debriefing interviews, it seems to happen at the socioemotional and affective realms as well as tangibly. Below, a situated representative case brings the phases described above to life.

A Situated Representation: Theatre of the Oppressed in Early Childhood Teacher Education

Employing Boal's Theatre of the Oppressed (Figure 7.1), we (Souto-Manning, Cahnmann-Taylor, Dice, & Wooten, 2008) sought to develop a process that would benefit teachers on an individual and contextual level. The following research questions guided the development of our approach to critical performative early childhood teacher education and guided our inquiry:

- Considering that teachers are socialized to speak, talk, and act in gendered, cultural, racial, and/or classed ways, how can embodying and problematizing oppression through spect-acting convey more depth and breadth to conflicts experienced by new teachers?
- In what ways might a critical performative approach provide unique contributions to early childhood teacher education?

To explore such questions, data were collected over a period of three years as part of a larger project to answer questions about effective practices for the recruitment and support of minority and nontraditional, bilingual pre- and in-service teachers (Cahnmann-Taylor, Rymes, & Souto-Manning, 2005; Rymes, Cahnmann-Taylor, & Souto-Manning, 2008).

Teachers were participants in a program named *Teachers for English Language Learners* (TELL) funded by the U.S. Department of Education Transition to Teaching Program. TELL was designed to recruit and support bilingual adults (TELL Scholars) to become K-12 teachers in Georgia high-need LEA (Local Education Associations). As we developed our performative model, we sought to support the retention of such highly qualified professionals in high-need public schools in light of the high rate of teacher burnout mentioned earlier in this chapter. Sessions employing the critical performative approach to early childhood teacher education happened once or twice per semester for three to six hours, from 2003 to 2009 (Cahnmann-Taylor & Souto-Manning, 2010). These performative focus groups involved between 30 and 40 pre-service and in-service teachers who were part of the TELL program. Specific workshops varied in number of participants—some were as small as five and some larger than 35.

In addition to the case presented in this chapter, there were several T.O. sessions during which we elicited oppressive circumstances for bilingual teachers and rehearsed them to explore alternative responses (Cahnmann-Taylor & Souto-Manning, 2010). The bilingual teachers are Protagonists in these scenes. Generative themes over the course of the project are represented by Figure 7.2. TELL Scholars represented the Antagonists in their own lives—these range from students in their classrooms, colleagues, paraprofessionals, parents, administrators and even us professors with whom they take certification coursework (Cahnmann-Taylor, Wooten, Souto-Manning, & Dice, 2009).

The case study presented in this chapter is that of a publicly funded full-day Pre-Kindergarten teacher named Sonia (pseudonym) whose participation in Theatre of the Oppressed for educators reflected common experiences of our critical performative approach to teacher education (Souto-Manning et al., 2008). While this study represents three scenes of interactions between teacher and assistant teacher, the corpus of data presents a variety of conflicts explored. Some of the conflicts presented occurred between teachers and assistant teachers, while others represented teachers, parents, students and administrators. The cases generated from early childhood educators of children aged zero to five only raised issues between lead teachers and assistant teachers as illustrated in Figure 7.2.

Boalian Theatre in Early Childhood Teacher Education

In this section, I present the case of Sonia, a Pre-Kindergarten teacher (Souto-Manning, Cahnmann-Taylor, Dice, & Wooten, 2008). This case

Generative Themes

Figure 7.2. Generative Themes (Cahnmann-Taylor, Wooten, Souto-Manning, & Dice, 2009).

represents the process of critical performative early childhood teacher education as applied to a very important and seldom discussed topic—the relationships and conflicts between lead teachers and assistant teachers in early childhood classrooms. Below, Sonia's words and actions are categorized according to the phases presented by Figure 7.1.

The Theatre of the Oppressed for educators workshops (Cahnmann-Taylor & Souto-Manning, 2010) portrayed in this chapter took place in the College of Education at the University of Georgia on a weekday between the hours of 5 and 8 pm. Four other newly-certified early childhood educators who were familiar with one another from various T. O. sessions were present, and took the role of spect-actors. All participants shared instances in which they had experienced recurring oppression in the professional realm. After relaying their narratives to the group, the participants decided on one narrative that was somehow representative of their own experiences and therefore would be meaningful and useful to each of them. They decided that Sonia presented a generative theme that could offer implications to all participants (Jensen, 1999).

Sonia was having difficulty with her Teaching Assistant (TA). As a result, she was under so much stress she was feeling physically ill and not interacting well with students. Sonia felt her TA did not fulfill her duties and that the TA undermined Sonia's authority in the classroom. She tried confronting the TA and talking to the principal but none of the solutions she tried yielded a satisfactory resolution. As she shared her struggle (phase 1: generative themes), many of the participants were able to relate to the situation and her dilemma was selected and codified (phase 2: codification).

(A) Generative Themes & Codification

Sonia was frequently put down and challenged by the Teaching Assistant who had more seniority than Sonia at the school where they worked. The more experienced assistant did not have the credentials to become a lead teacher, yet considered herself more knowledgeable. As Sonia described the situation of recurring oppression, she first described the TA's actions she felt were inappropriate. Sonia's description of her situation follows. Please note that the pronoun "she" signifies the TA.

Sonia: It all starts in the morning, when she comes in. It has been going on every morning. She and her daughter, who does an internship in the school in a different teacher's room, come in. The first thing: they come in and go to the computer and start e-mailing. The kids are there and they just ignore them.

Sonia went on to describe her attempts at confronting the TA, asking the TA for help, and that the TA compared Sonia to previous lead teachers, thereby showing the group that the TA would not engage in discussion with her about making change.

Sonia: When she comes and intimidates so much that I say only half the things I have to say. I want to say "this is it." I gotta talk to her. So, I even typed up the general job expectations for her, during this time I want you to do this and this and that. Then she comes in that morning and I said, "good morning" and she didn't say good morning. Her daughter said good morning and my TA just looked at me like, "What's the problem?" And I said, "I don't like it. The minute you guys come in, you go to the computer. I don't think that's professional." And she said, "But there's nobody coming in." And I said, "But my kids are here." And then they just both left the room. And they never came back. And then the next day she didn't come back. And then she came back the following Monday and we had an okay day.

Identifying with Sonia's experience, the group of new teachers decided to codify Sonia's oppressive experience into three scenes and (re)enact the situation. They clearly recognized the prominence of this problematic interaction, which is common in early childhood classrooms — conflictual dynamics between lead teachers and assistant teachers. Sonia's situation was framed in light of cultural beliefs and academic practices. Culturally, those more experienced are typically recognized as more knowledgeable. Yet, academically one's degree and credentials determine formal hierarchical relationships in the Pre-K classroom.

In further describing the teaching assistant, Sonia presented the following interactions, representing multiple realms in which Sonia experienced oppression:

(1) The TA took charge and told Sonia what to do. She compared Sonia to previous lead teachers and drew on her longer tenure in their school:

TA: Why don't you put those chairs down? The other teachers did it—the other teachers that came before you.

The Teaching Assistant developed expectations based on her previous experiences. Having longer tenure at the school, she believed that she knew what Sonia was to do. When her expectations and Sonia's behaviors did not match, she questioned Sonia's actions and drew on her knowledge of what experienced former teachers did, referring to the "other teachers that came before." Sonia felt oppressed by criticisms from the Teaching Assistant and her prescriptions about how to behave and what to do.

(2) The TA also developed relationships with children's parents and talked negatively about Sonia to those parents.

Sonia: I was really concerned about the trust issue. She said things to parents that undermined my ability to teach. She was telling them that, "Oh, she's already changed her daily schedule three times." Like that's some indication of inability or lack of experience. Whenever I tried to adjust to the reality, tried to make it better, she didn't see that I was trying to do better. She saw these changes as insecurity, and she spoke ill of me about those things to parents.

Sonia felt oppressed by the comments this TA was making to the parents of students in her classroom and saw such comments undermining her role as lead teacher. Embodying concepts learned in her teacher education program, Sonia sought to reflect on observations in order to teach responsively. Nevertheless, cultural expectations regarding the role of a teacher differed. While Sonia was trying to be responsive to the needs of the children in her classroom, the Teaching Assistant was more concerned with structure and consistency.

(3) Another pattern Sonia recognized in her interactions with her TA was that they had different ideas about their roles in the classroom.

Sonia: I said, "I consider that your job." And she said, "Your job ex-
        pectation is different."

In the excerpt above, Sonia articulated to the TA the expectations
of the job to be performed by a lead teacher and expectations of a
Teaching Assistant in the early education classroom.

(5) Sonia also recognized that they had different beliefs about how to
    interact with children.

Sonia: She even told me that I'm too nice to the kids, and I said, "That's
        my way of dealing with the little children. That's the way I
        teach the children." But, her assertion was that I'm just a will-
        ing victim and, you know, that I just try to please the children,
        not teaching them.

Finally, Sonia articulated their different beliefs regarding children's development and appropriate interactional styles. While these
beliefs are culturally based, this excerpt represents one more point of
tension.

As Sonia shared her narrative, multiple tensions were identified.
Together with the group of early educators in our study, Sonia identified the most recursive and representative situation as number 1
above in which the TA told Sonia what to do and compared her to
previous lead teachers. Together, the participants of the group codified Sonia's experience of oppression into three scenes, which were
reenacted several times with different actions and reactions to determine what Sonia's performative options were in moments of interactional conflict.

(B) Spect-Acting and Reality Check

Following deconstruction, the acting was recast in three scenes. Sonia,
two teacher educators, and four other early educators acted as spect-
actors (a hybrid of spectator and actor). At any point in time, any
spect-actor could replace the Protagonist or Antagonist in the scene
and performatively provide a new perspective.

The scenes acted were as follows:

Scene 1: Teaching Assistant ignored Sonia's and the children's needs upon entry to the classroom.

Scene 2: Sonia made a request to the TA for help.

Scene 3: The TA compared Sonia to a previous teacher seeking to exemplify how good teachers act.

The perspectives and possible solutions the spect-actors first offered emphasized concrete actions for solving the problem. Several spect-actors performed Sonia documenting the TA's behaviors in various ways (with a notepad, hidden video camera, etc.) in order to garner support from the school principal or to secure evidence to have the TA removed from Sonia's classroom, moved to another school, or fired. Alternatively, an early educator performed Sonia offering the TA explicit instructions about her role in order to make her expectations clearer. Sonia engaged in a reality check with the group by questioning the feasibility of such solutions and explained why such performed solutions would not work in her particular situation. She further refined the codified generative theme and identified the underlying issue between her and her TA as an issue of power. The group changed the focus of their suggestions as individuals took Sonia's (the Protagonist's) place and attempted to work on the power dynamics and differentials in her interactions with the TA.

First, spect-actors suggested using *strategic subordination*. Here, Sonia pretended that she was playing along. As the scene was reenacted, Sonia again engaged in reality checks about their suggestions, further refining details of the situation. The spect-actors who took her place (early childhood teachers and teacher educators) acted out several scenes. The scenes presented below are representative examples. Behaviors (such as laughter and nods) are indicated between double parentheses.

Scene 1: Enacted by an early childhood teacher, Sonia, and a teacher educator.

Spect-actor 1 as Sonia: Oh, you smell good today. And I like your dress too. What's her name? Whatever. Miss.

Joker: How realistic is that?

Sonia: Oh, she doesn't care.

((laughter))

Sonia: And she wears like, she's a big lady and she wears like jerseys and stuff.

((laughter))

Sonia: Yeah, yeah, you know that's like obviously not real.

In Scene 1, Sonia clearly stated that pretending to play along would not work within this specific interactional context. While another Teaching Assistant might play niceties, according to her previous experience and to the context of the situation, this TA was not going to play along. So, while a solution was offered, the reality check haltered its applicability. Nevertheless, participants saw that pretending to play along could potentially be a solution to a situation of conflict and/or oppression. This strategy (*strategic subordination*) was suggested again and again across cases over the years.

Scene 2 below presents another solution which entails suggesting another attempt at strategic subordination. In this reenactment, the proposed solution was to attempt to blur the roles of teacher and Teaching Assistant.

Scene 2: Enacted by two early childhood teachers and Sonia

Spect-actor 5:	I'm going on the fact that you're saying that she thinks that she's a lead teacher, right?
Sonia:	Mm-hm.
Spect-actor 5 as Sonia:	Uhm. I really don't know how to do this, can you?
Spect-actor 3 as TA:	But they pay you.
Spect-actor 5 as Sonia:	Yeah, but right now I'm really having difficulty with this part of it. So, do you think you can help me in any way?
Spect-actor 3 as TA:	I'm here. I assist you.
Spect-actor 5 as Sonia:	I mean because you've been in the school for five years or six years or whatever.

Spect-actor 3 as TA: I assist you.

Spect-actor 5 as Sonia: Yeah. Can I assist you?

Spect-actor 3 as TA: Oh, it would be wonderful.

Again, upon reality check, this was not deemed as an applicable or possible solution. Yet, it did not seem as artificial as the solution previously presented.

Scene 3 presents a follow-up to the suggestion presented in Scene 2. Upon debriefing by the Joker (teacher educator), Sonia seemed to think that this could be real and applicable to her situation. Collaboration rather than competition for power and legitimacy was deemed acceptable by Sonia.

Scene 3:   Enacted by a teacher educator

Joker: Have you ever traded places? Because she thinks she's the teacher. Has she ever really led the classroom for a morning? If you went to her, for example, she's walking in and you can say even after school, "Well, tomorrow I'd like to propose that you lead the classroom because you have some experience with pre-K and I will do your job and try to assist you."

Spect-actors also suggested and acted out extreme possibilities for change. These interactions often lead to laughter. Indeed, parody is useful in such situations of distress to diffuse the seriousness of a situation. Sonia described the experience of parody in acting as adding to her increasing comfort in dealing with such a difficult situation.

Sonia: I might not agree with everything, but, it was, there's a comical touch too, that helped me relax about the real situation.

Besides *strategic subordination* (pretending to play along), and *parody* (refusing to play along), other strategies were articulated in various situations over the years. Some of them include: *calling authority* (e.g., summon a principal), *keeping documentation* (e.g., anecdotal notes, video footage), *enduring the situation* (often for a limited amount of time), *forming networks, consensual subordination* (playing along), and *explicit insubordination* (which often yields a parodic rendering). While not all of these are presented in this chapter, they were strategies performatively enacted again and again (Cahnmann-Taylor & Souto-Manning, 2010).

(C) Action

Action occurred in this case study through the lead teacher's subjective self-awareness, sense of empowerment, and new behaviors in the classroom. By acting out her experiences with the TA, Sonia identified patterns of interaction (e.g., competition, bids for power and knowledge) that may have perpetuated the oppressive situation. The hierarchy set up by the school district was seen as problematic by the Teaching Assistant who had more experience but fewer professional credentials. Confronting this issue and approaching such an interaction with the TA was problematic and nerve-wracking for Sonia. Upon request from one of the early educators, she showed the group what she looked like when she was interacting with the TA, thus bringing the physical embodiment of the situation to the forefront.

The group suggested that she change the way she presented herself when she interacted with her TA in order to convey a position of strength. Initially, when interacting with the TA, Sonia's posture slumped; she frowned, and looked down at the floor. Her peers noticed that her low voice and posture were positioning her as insecure, and non-agentive in the interaction. By standing taller and relaxing her facial muscles, Sonia immediately felt a difference. The interaction below presents some of the suggestions for changing the body language and Sonia's reactions to them. The interaction is carried on by two early childhood educators and Sonia.

Spect-actor 1:   Put your hands to your hips. Every time. Like your hands and arms are up. It's making you higher. Your hands are higher than she is.

Sonia: Oh really? I never heard of that. This is good. Okay. See if I can get bigger.

((Sonia tries suggested body positioning))

Spect-actor 2: Yes, you need to make yourself big.
Sonia: Oh, that makes sense. It feels better.

While the suggestion to merely change her body language was the only one Sonia felt was realistic during the focus group, she later reflected on her experience in the group as helpful because it was less solution-focused and more process-oriented. She now felt there was something she could do. She changed her own stance, something of which she had control.

Following is her rendering of the situation and her reflections on the critical performative teacher education process in which she had engaged according to a debriefing interview conducted months after her situation was critically reenacted. She recounted the process and the learnings of the performative focus group. She also talked about returning to the focus group setting as a support structure that helped monitor the progress of one's situation.

Sonia: What do I do? I bring my problem there. I act out my problem. I reveal myself, one layer after another and just peel the anxiety. I let other people have it. And we share our emotions together, problems together, act it out. Sometimes you just don't need words; you just use your body language and let all the problems out ((laughs)). And we discuss and seek the possible solutions together. And after each possibility, we act it out again. Until you feel comfortable with some of those solutions that can help you deal with the problem afterwards. You come back again and discuss the progress, and act out again. And you are relieved from your anxiety and you learn from the process. And you feel better and you gradually solve the problem, or release it. At least, you release the intensity and tension of the conflict and you do better.

She further described the effects of participating in critical performative early childhood teacher education.

Sonia: It was actually empowering for me to see different ways to deal with the problems.

Interviewer: What do you mean by empowering?

Sonia: Because I'm really subjective and then, I can only see one way, if I am focused on "Why, why, why?" But then, there are different reactions here and there, so I need to open up and widen my view, and there might be a reason or reaction coming from my TA, even if I'm the same person. If I see differently, say it differently, and, you know, act differently, show different body language, she might, you know, show a different side of her too. So, human beings have, you know, a lot of different sides, a wide range of thinking, so, we respond differently to different actions. Now I know that. So, yeah, it was kind of an empowering experience, yes.

Sonia went on to acknowledge the process of opening up options and considering multiple strategies.

Sonia: During the focus group, there are lots of options that you can think of, you know, some are realistic, some are not. But, you know, that gives you a lot of strategies that, "Oh! This might work. That might work."

So, regardless of the reality of any one specific solution to the situation presented, Sonia articulated the need to consider the multiple facets of the human being with whom she was in conflict. She embraced the concept of humility. "Humility helps us to understand this obvious truth: No one knows it all; no one is ignorant of everything" (Freire, 1998, p. 39). Recognizing that she did not know all the facets and motives influencing the Teaching Assistant's actions helped her better navigate their interactions.

Sonia articulated the importance of developing a repertoire of options to deal with oppressive situations. Instead of feeling immediately oppressed, she could refer to these strategies and think, "Oh! This might work. That might work" as articulated above. This repertoire can serve to detract stress from situations that might otherwise be oppressive.

Discussion and Reflections

Using a performative critical approach early childhood teacher education, such as the one described in this chapter, opens up options for addressing issues common to teachers. Because there are multiple educators in the early childhood classroom, different points of view about roles, teaching, and children are common. Sonia's case highlights several of these common themes. Teachers can benefit not only from the support of a group and a feeling of collectivity but also from the process of reflecting on patterns of interaction, deconstructing them performatively, considering multiple (re)actions and rehearsing transformative actions.

Discussion

As reported by Sonia during a debriefing interview, although acting can be challenging at first, it can ultimately be energizing and offer a way to diffuse the intensity of conflict-ridden situations. It can also provide possibilities for constant reality checks. Several months after Sonia's case was acted out, there was a change in her language about the situation. She changed from talking about her situation as one in which she was helpless and not in control to talking about it agentively.

When Sonia first presented her case she made statements about feeling insecure. She described her heart pounding out of her chest and that she really "suffered." Months later, she said:

> I think I was more than ready to go to work instead of, "Okay, how do I deal with this lady again?" Instead of that, "Okay, I can get through this one. I am a powerful person." So, that was great.

Sonia's case highlights the use of performative critical teacher education in accounting and allowing for different worldviews and specific contexts. She said, "Some suggestions were just unrealistic for me." Traditional teacher models may not be able to tend to the nuances of individualities, cultural practices and personality traits. What works for one person may or may not work for everyone everywhere.

Performing culture circles allows for recognition of multiple assumptions and presumptions in teaching and a realization that differing worldviews are not personal affronts. It opens up the possibilities for using the teachers' very experiences as cases to be performatively analyzed and interactionally explored. Such a performative approach has the potential to open up possibilities for addressing diversities in the teacher education classroom and in early childhood education in general, as it offers teachers tools for considering multiple perspectives and worldviews.

Sonia's case also highlights the importance of body language in interaction. Teachers act and use their bodies in all of their interactions. The performative aspect of T.O. creates a space for teachers to explore their bodies and positionings in teaching and interacting with others. Sonia recounted the experience of embodying her interactions in the context of T.O. as liberating for her and influential on her future interactions with her TA.

Sonia: I was kind of intimidated a lot, but I wasn't really aware of my body language, what it shows and communicates to her at the time. But I realized that the way I was responding to her helped her to treat me that way a lot more. It was a powerful moment. I had to realize, to see the situation.

Later she recounted her newfound personal awareness:

Sonia: I am really aware of what I'm doing. I know I'm not doing that anymore. In the classroom with my TA especially. This is a gradual learning process. And I am really aware of my speech pattern, and I always try to improve.

The experience of acting might also offer a potentially comfortable atmosphere and lighter mood for exploring tense situations. In the excerpt below, Sonia articulated the importance of considering interactional contexts in such performative approaches, which are hypothesized in cases that might only be read in teacher education classrooms. She addressed the difference in acting out a problem versus talking about it. The importance and power of real-time interaction in an unknown situation (as each spect-actor does not know in advance how others will react) is one of the factors that makes such an approach so useful and powerful.

> Sonia: Acting it makes it easier to express. I mean, if you have to act out the real situation, you know. Sometimes, when you are talking about situations, you worry, "Ooh, what would people think?" You might, you know, worry about other people's opinions. But "Oh, this is acting out." And, I think it's a little bit more comfortable than just talking about the truth because it represents everyone, or it tries to.

In the excerpt above, Sonia explained that despite her initial discomfort with acting, she saw its benefits, as it considers interactions and reactions from multiple perspectives. Additionally, it allowed for reality checks and constant refining (and redefining) of the situation. Even when discussing one's specific situation, Sonia expressed that she saw more room for misunderstanding in talking. Despite her initial discomfort, she felt more comfortable in an acting situation, as it represented the perspectives of the Protagonist and explored reasons behind the actions of the Antagonist. In addition, by demechanizing the body and examining its role in education and interpersonal interaction, there was a dimension added to the possibilities for rehearsing the revolution and constructing change. Through performing culture circles, teachers may come to explore ways to use the language of the body and utilize it in social and/or professional interactions.

Reflections on Practice

Long work hours and the high demands of early childhood teaching lead to challenges in offering this kind of critical performative approach to in-service teacher education. Such in-services are often held after school hours or on weekends. I propose (as illustrated by Sonia's reflection below and by many other teachers) that T.O. offers a more energized and playful situation than traditional in-service teacher education sessions (Tom, 1997). Indeed, Sonia described the unique

characteristic of T.O. having a different feel than other teacher training. Upon being asked about the challenges of this training, Sonia re-
layed:

> ...the time and coming out when I'm tired, that's the only thing.
> But it's well worth coming to the group. Because even if your
> body is tired, you leave energized in your spirit, so it's well worth
> coming.

A critical performative approach to early childhood teacher education opens up possibilities, spaces for transformative action. The
process of exploring conflict through theatre may be experienced as
relieving rather than adding greater stress. Sonia recounted:

> I feel relieved that sometimes you have built up emotions here.
> And then, with encouragement and support from the group, you
> can just let it out one layer after another layer. And suddenly you
> feel like a different person!

So, reflecting on the practical aspects of employing performative
critical early childhood teacher education, we find that it allows
teachers to feel energized and less stressed as they leave, which is the
opposite of so many professional development instances from which
teachers adjourn with a long list of things to do. Like Sonia, teachers
participating in this kind of professional development may be able to
release stressful emotions and leave with greater conflict management
skills in addition to feeling like a different person, energized and re-
freshed.

Implications

As there are multiple solutions proposed by spect-actors to Sonia's
situation, likewise there are many implications of being socialized
into this kind of critical performative teacher education. Day in and
day out, early childhood educators experience conflict, whether it is
in interactions with a parent, administrator, assistant teacher, or student. Being socialized in habitual ways of speaking and acting in cer-

tain cultural circumstances, such as rigid interactional patterns and the culturally based beliefs regarding the needs of children in early education classrooms (Freire, 1970; Rogoff, 2003) can hinder an early childhood educator's ability to consider multiple perspectives and needs in a moment of struggle. Instead of creating a "me against them" situation, embodying conflict through acting can convey more depth and breadth to the nature of a conflict, offering an array of solutions that may ultimately allow the early childhood educator to consider various actions that can modify a problematic situation.[5]

---

[5] For more about Boalian theatre in teacher education, please read Cahnmann-Taylor, M., & Souto-Manning, M. (2010). *Teachers act up!* New York: Teachers College Press.

Part III:

On the Power
and Possibilities of
Freirean Culture Circles

CHAPTER 8

On Praxis

...for Freire dialogue—what he refers to elliptically as 'speaking true words'—is a praxis which contains the two dimensions of reflection and action as they are combined in transforming the world...[N]ot only is dialogue essentially creative and transformative, it is both an existential necessity and a methodology (dialogics) for overcoming oppression.

(Peters & Lankshear, 1994, p. 188)

Authentic dialogue in which teacher and learner roles are dialectically blurred, negotiated and renegotiated is a key component of Freirean culture circles. According to Paulo Freire (2004), "dialogue is the opportunity available to me to open up to the thinking of others and thereby not wither away in isolation" (p. 103). Honoring Freire's intention, this chapter opens up to the dialogue and thinking of culture circle participants featured throughout this book.

Freire (1998) proposed that humility is a basic human condition necessary to embrace authentic dialogue, recognizing that no one knows everything there is to know while at the same time no one is ignorant of everything. Every person has something to say, a contribution to make. Freirean pedagogy seeks to promote transformation using dialogue as a tool to name, problematize, challenge, and change oppressive situations. According to Peters and Lankshear (1994), Freire embraced:

> ...a critical hermeneutics which is both ontological and epistemological. As ontological it is tied to Freire's conviction that our vocation as human beings is to become more fully human. It is epistemological in that Freire offers a methodology for investigating generative themes, as part of the praxis through which humans become more fully human. In both its (unified) ontological and epistemological aspects this hermeneutics is *critical*. It is critical because we are called on to perform *evaluative* acts in the praxis of naming the world. (p. 188)

Freire's ontological conviction is evident throughout this book as teachers (read facilitators) seek to become more fully human, more vulnerable, and learn alongside their students from a humble stance. Responding to his call to recreate and reinvent his pedagogy (Macedo & Freire, 1998) instead of importing a fixed curriculum, through re-creating Freire's critical approach across contexts in Brazil and in the United States, children and adults introduced in this book had and continue to have the opportunity to embrace praxis. According to Mayo (1999),

> Praxis...lies at the heart of Freire's approach, which often entails the process of 'codification and decodification' whereby elements related to the social reality of the...learner are objectified in such a way that they can be perceived in a partly detached and more critical manner. The concept, entailing an ongoing process of transformative action and reflection, is a recurring one in Freire's writings. (p. 91)

This very same concept became clear as participants recounted their experiences with culture circles as they shared the lessons learned and reflected on the process and resulting actions. Therefore, embracing dialogics as method, I conclude the book offering you an invitation to engage with the voices of Freire, Ayers, Fine, Giroux, Goulet, Greene, Weis, and the culture circle participants dialoguing with one another. They all embrace a pedagogy of hope as a framework toward overcoming oppression and transforming the world.

Reflections and Action: Lessons from Participants

Cut off from practice, theory becomes a simple verbalism. Separated from theory, practice is nothing but blind activism. That is why there is no authentic praxis   outside   the   dialectical   unity,   action-reflection,   practice-theory...[R]eflection is only legitimate when it sends us back...to the concrete context where it seeks to clarify the facts. In doing so, reflection renders our action more effective over against those facts. In throwing light on an accomplished action, or one that is being accomplished, authentic reflection clarifies future action, which in its given time will have to be open to renewed reflection. (Freire, 1985, p. 156)

Culture Circles: A Transformative Approach to Education

A culture circle is a group of individuals involved in learning...as well as in the political analysis of their immediate reality and national interests. In culture circles, reading demands more than decodification of linguistic symbols. It is viewed as political "reading" of the world. (Giroux, 1985, p. viii)

Mollie: I think that the teacher culture circle really encouraged the strengths-based perspective with the idea that if you want teachers to grow and develop but just point your finger at them saying, "this is what you're really doing poorly you should've improved this, this and this," as opposed to the strengths-based perspective, like coming to teachers saying "you've done a really great job, and this is your strength, this is what you're doing really well, and how do you think we can develop that more?" it's not going to work. Focusing on the strengths, on what teachers are doing is so much more empowering and encouraging to them. I learned a lot from this and will continue to use that in my classroom.

Hillary: Yes, it's totally different, than anything I've been a part of. I wish that we had this earlier 'cause I think it would've helped teachers kind of manage their stress, change things in their classrooms and beyond and get through difficult times. But it has been totally different from like, professional development. In the circle you were really learning, and usually in professional development you just sit there and listen to somebody else talk.

Marilyn: I loved it.

Mollie: ((laughs))

Marilyn: Even though, like we did have to stay later on, Monday, Monday night.

James: It was Monday night. Yea.

Marilyn: Um, and so, 'cause usually on Monday, we'd be all like, oh, it's Monday, let's go to the study group. Once we got there, it was such a relief. We got to talk, to listen, to realize what other classes were doing. Some of what they're doing is the same stuff what we were doing. Some of the things I wish I could change were the same. I think it was really assuring also, in that aspect of being able to think about and acting to change things.

James: I agree, even like, I think everyone felt isolated from everybody else.

Marilyn: Uh-hum ((nods))

James: And in the school, even in the small school like this, we just felt very isolated. So, just getting to know teachers that I've been working with for years, you know. Just like, oh, I didn't realize you did that, and, I didn't realize you did this. And, it was really nice, it was, it was like, giant, um, kind o' like talk-back, like we all had opportunities to talk to each other, learn what everyone's doing, learn what everyone else was getting overwhelmed by. Knowing that you were not alone felt very good. It was no longer my issue, it was a collective issue. I mean, 'cause you know, sometimes it feels like a hermetically sealed bubble, but we'd all be in our offices going, oh, why do I need to do this? Ugh, I got to do this paper work. I mean, I know that other people were thinking the same thing, but just quietly alone in their office. And now, together we could speak up, we could ask questions and we could negotiate what was important and why or why not.

((chuckles))

Marilyn: And then when we came together, like, oh, wow, you thought the same thing, so.

Corry: We were able to change things, or help each other, and problem solve together.

James: Or learn what other techniques they have to change this oppressive situation.

Marilyn: Right. Like, some people would say, oh, I did it this way, and I am like, I hadn't thought of that, you know. Or, I did it this way and it felt better, more manageable, and I like this way and see how it works. Sometimes we worked to change the situation, but sometimes we came to see ways in which reacting differently to a situation, to something we had to do changed things around. The group helped keep things in perspective. It was just great, it was just great, it was great for feedback, I looked totally forward to it.

Mollie: It was a place to talk about your job as a preschool teacher. As a preschool teacher there were things that I needed to talk about, address, and there's just no time for this in your job. The job doesn't really allow for it. Like there's not, there's not time set, a part of the day, just to talk through, to dialogue about some of the stuff that you don't want to talk about, but that you need to. Your job didn't necessarily give you time to do that; the teacher study group, our culture circle did.

Hillary: ((nodding)) It was a place, too, where we could talk about any issues that we were having, especially those that we thought were like outside of our control, like rules and regulations, how it affects the classroom, things like that. And we tried to problem solve together. Many times, we just kind of had to figure out how to deal with them or to make our lives easier. We may not have changed the regulations, but we changed how they affected our classrooms and our lives.

Corry: I think that the overall feeling is why I kept coming back, is that I never went away um thinking that was a waste of my time.

Mollie: Right.

Corry: I always felt like either I found something that would change things for me, or that I helped somebody to find some solutions for them, for their situation. Just through our discussion, and dialogue, the whole dynamic, we all felt free to talk and could say whatever we wanted to say, and that freedom just really allowed us to really get to the heart of what the issues were—what anyone should know, or wanted to help with. The dialogue gave us freedom to offer our opinion and to engage in planning and carrying out our actions, to change things in our classrooms individually or together.

The Facilitator: Roles and Strategies

...the decodification by a "culture circle" under the self-effacing stimulus of a coordinator who is no "teacher" in the conventional sense, but who has become an educator-educatee—in dialogue with educatee-educators too often treated by formal educators as passive recipients of knowledge (Goulet, 2005, p. viii).

James: Mariana was the facilitator of the teacher group, but she really would follow our leads, ask questions that helped us move ahead and look deeper at situations. So, I mean, originally, we're discussing literacy, issues that she had brought from our classrooms, and how we could change things, what pressures are keeping us from moving ahead, from progressing in our vision and practice. But then there was a shift. I remember going to a meeting and another teacher saying, I've got to talk about this right now, you know, and so, after making sure the issue was important, it was present in our classrooms, we just kind of sat down and she kind of laid her problem out, and we just, each of us questioned, talked about it. We asked questions like "why do you think this is happening?" to see what forces were influencing the situation. Then, we problem solved together—maybe if we try this, you know. I think it was beneficial for the teacher and for us to problem solve together with our peers.

Marilyn: So, the person helping us come together to ask questions about what was going on in our classrooms really cared. She did not know everything and did not give us a laundry list of all the things we needed to do. Like yesterday, she spent time observing me and going, oh, well, I love how you are doing this, this is a really great strategy that you're doing here, you know, um, and how you're promoting critical literacy in your classroom. It was like she was learning with us and then, bringing some things that mattered to everyone to the table, I mean, to the circle.

Jill: But I remember that she was also flexible. When we were ready to step in and offer our issues, she would step back. Maybe she had answers to the things we were discussing, but she asked lots of questions that made us think instead of telling us you should do this and that.

Hillary: Yes, so sometimes we might have a topic, a theme coming into it, but sometimes it didn't materialize because of an issue somebody else might bring might be more urgent to the group. As a group, we kind of fell in and decided, okay this is what we want to talk about this week, or we talk about this issue that we are dealing with. But we needed to be honest and talk about hard issues, not using this group decision making process to avoid talking about those issues. She helped us remember this. This was not just like a social chitchat, it was real problem solving.

Shante: Sometimes we talked about issues that we needed to learn more about. Mariana helped organize resources, both readings and people, to provide us more information so that our dialogue could be an informed one. We couldn't ask questions, uncover the issues if we were not aware of the issues.

Jill: So, we might abandon our initial theme, but I felt like it was one of those things where Mariana would tell us, okay this is what we can talk about, but so and so has this, should we talk about this? And so she would feel up the group and see what the group felt we needed to address that night, more urgently.

Marilyn: When I think about the way she was facilitating, I think she was an excellent facilitator, like I tried to think about having the same study group with someone else and not her. And I don't think it would be nearly as good just because of how open she was to letting the conversation go wherever it needed to go, always asking questions, though, that took us places we didn't necessarily want but needed to go.

James: But I think it was excellent in the sense that it didn't start out as open, like tell me your issues. Trust was developed.

Shante: And respect.

James: It didn't start out as open, so you didn't feel like you're walking out on a tight rope. You didn't feel like you had to bring a lot to it. At the very beginning, she would come in, and share some things we could relate to; like things that affected our classrooms, our teaching, but not talking about us directly. Then as we started feeling comfortable, she would share different things that she would see in the classrooms from watching the videotape or observing from the booth, and then she wouldn't say where, I think, but what she saw. And by having that start off, we engaged in the discussion of a topic that was affecting our lives as teachers. Then we eventually, all the participants, became comfortable enough to, um, you know, bring your own subject matter to the table, and I think that was very smart. But what she [the facilitator] did, I think, going from talking about issues that were important to us, that were real in our classrooms, made us want to come back. When she first invited us, she got to know our classrooms. You know, if at the very beginning she'd said, oh, whatever you wanna talk about, I think that we've all, we'd all 'ave gone, um, I like kids, you know ((chuckles)), or it would become a giant gripe session, and, we'd never gone anywhere critical, we'd not seen how we have the power to change things. I think it eventually became a problem solving session, a peer problem solving process that valued different voices, voices from the classrooms.

Corry: So, she modeled ways to teach in our own classroom while helping us deal with stressful situations.

The Process

…whereas banking education anesthetizes and inhibits creative power, problem-solving education involves a constant unveiling of reality. The former attempts to maintain submersion of consciousness; the latter strives for the emergence of consciousness and critical intervention in reality…problem-posing education which accepts neither a "well-behaved" present nor a pre-determined future…[problem-posing education] roots itself in the dynamic present and becomes revolutionary. (Freire, 1970, pp. 68-72)

Hillary: It provided a space, a way, an outlet for us to use, to talk about problems and issues in our classrooms. It was really good to hear all the ideas, what will be used, and good to hear that teachers actually have the similar issues in their classrooms. We came together, asked questions, tried to see what the problem was, and moved to problem solving together.

Mollie: You know, recognizing that these were shared issues and that we could problem solve together reinforced that it was a worthy amount of time. I think just talking about it and recognizing that we are not alone is therapeutic—not feeling isolated, alone. Issues that we all experienced were brought to the circle. Just the normal school day wasn't allowing us the opportunity to talk with your co-teachers about what's going on in and across the classrooms, and problem solve. When you are not talking about it you feel like, am I the only one who sees this, am I the only one who feels this way? And the teacher group was really therapeutic in that way, just to be able to recognize how common and prevalent some of the issues were. But if I were going, this is a really big issue, and I don't know what to do, and you go into the circle and everyone else's saying I don't know what to do either, even with that, we don't necessarily have to have solutions to the problem, but it was nice knowing that you weren't alone.

Lexy: And then we could talk and try to find answers together. We knew that many times there aren't the perfect answers or simple solutions for situations, and what works in one setting may not work in another. But recognizing that if this is going on in my classroom and in another, then teachers can collaborate and problem solve together and feel like we can do it instead of feeling like there is no way, this is not for me, I am a horrible teacher.

Shante: Yeah, problem solving through collaboration ((nodding)). It was really nice just 'cause it was very open, and you know if you had a problem, there was actually at least one other teacher who dealt with that, who can try to find solutions together, even if we knew that the same solution may not work as well in different classrooms.

Corry: It wasn't just a place to take problems or talk about what's great in our classroom, but also a place where we can get to know one another. It was a place that allowed us to get to know each other as people, on a more personal level, and to get to know more about their needs and wants, issues, and goals. Because we cared about each other, we were invested in the process. To talk and try to find solutions, to ask hard questions, required trust and close relationships.

James: One of the powerful things is that we did not oversimplify the process. After we talked and found some solutions, we would follow up and see what had worked, what had not, talk about the whys and if it had not worked. That became a theme to be addressed by the group all over again.

Marilyn: But instead of getting upset about it, we knew that it was part of the process.

A Safe Community of Learners

> Freire sought to create educational spaces...both a community of learners and a community of researchers, in which "facts" were submitted to analysis, "causes" reconsidered, and indeed "responsibility" reconceived in critical biographic, political, and historical context. The task, then, was not merely to educate us all to "what is," but to provoke analysis of "what has been" and release, as Maxine Greene would invite, our imagination for "what could be. (Weis & Fine, 2004, p. 109)

James: One of the first things that Mariana [the facilitator] said was, this is not about teacher bashing, which I think, totally just like, made us go oh, okay. And it's like a whole wave of fear was removed.

Corry: I definitely feel that our guard was let down and we could share anything that we wanted to, and we knew we wouldn't be looked down upon for thinking this, or we wouldn't be reprimanded. You know what I mean? It was a very safe place, and I think one of the biggest memories I have is of people getting emotional, even crying about something that was going on. And I was like, wow, they really feel strongly about that. And just knowing that it stopped there, and people won't go like, oh, do you know that so and so was crying in the teacher culture circle last night, you know what I mean?

James: Right, it wasn't that gossiping that usually happens.

Marilyn: It was a good time to meet other teachers, to see what they're about, 'nd all that. I felt isolated. Knowing who everyone was, what they cared about was important. We were not just teachers, but we were people with likes and dislikes. So, getting to know my co-workers as people, I really enjoyed that part of it too. Because of these relationships, because we trusted each other, we felt safe to let our guard down.

Lexy: It was okay to feel vulnerable, to not know, to be angry.

Marilyn: It was like a safe place for us to meet and talk about stuff. We weren't afraid of being looked down upon, or we got a problem with something. It was real open.

James: Oh yeah, I totally agree with that. I think also the fact that, it was an open space, but we developed trust before we were asked to take personal risks.

Lexy: I think so. It was a safe haven. But it wasn't a place people crossed their arms. They put up their sleeves and got to work, talking and asking questions, and looking for solutions, and supporting each other. But the same people who comforted you, pushed you. It was that kind of place.

Marilyn: I feel closer to those teachers than I do to the teachers who were not in the culture circle, 'cause I feel like we shared that. You know, we kind o' put ourselves out there, and they were real receptive and, you know, understanding 'nd all that.

James: It was like the confessionary, a place where there were mysteries shared ((laughs)).

Marilyn: And they all got to be solved. Not by some other person or miracle, but by us.

Jill: It was like a support group, a place where the teachers go where it's kind o' like a safe area, where, um, we can just talk about different things going on as well as learn from each other and problem solve together. I felt more than anything that you can share ideas more openly, more freely.

Hillary: It was a safe place, and I felt that it gave me a sense of community as we decided what we're working toward. I found it special, I got to know everybody and liked how we were working together to make things better.

James: Mariana [the facilitator] really set it up from the get-go, she set this up as a safe place. I think everyone was pretty tied up. I mean like, everyone asked, what do you guys do, you know, what do you do? Why do you want to stay after hours on Mondays? And I remember saying, oh, we just talked about teacher issues, and would just kind of drop it

there, you know? We all had great respect for that group of
people and for the space it created.

Shante: I think that was probably one of the best things is that you
felt comfortable enough to talk about anything in there. And
you know, you didn't have to worry about, oh, if I say this
somebody is going to go tell it to someone else. There was
trust. If I am having trouble with something or someone, I
could be sincere, and people would talk and together give
you strategies. I didn't have to worry about somebody going
back and saying this is what was said, so it was very open
and it was very helpful. I remember there were a couple of
things that I had brought in and was asking about. I walked
away feeling that okay I can totally handle this now. I know,
you know, they gave me these possible solutions to try out,
recognizing that they might work or might not. But these solutions were often better than anything any of us could come
up with on our own because we thought of complicating factors as we talked about solutions.

Corry: It was not like stuffy staff meetings, where you always sit
there, sit on your hands, and bite your tongue. It was not a
place where you are being told what to do. Everyone was
learning and everyone had something to say. It was really a
place just to open up. While there were tensions when questions were being asked, there was respect. I felt that tension
among our group was dealt with in helpful ways. I honestly
think that everyone felt that way. Sometimes, someone
would come in there not even knowing that they needed to
talk about something. As issues were brought up, so many
times we could relate that power struggle with our own
situations, and were able to talk, really listen, learn, problem
solve and feel better.

Shante: This was so helpful, being part of this community. I mean all
the other professional training that I've done 'as been so bor-
ing, and it's like somebody stands up there and just preaches
at you. You don't get to say anything, you don't get to do

anything, you just sit there and have to take it in and at the end of it, be like okay, none of that is pertaining to me. So, this was a group thing. We went around and talked, and so EVERYTHING, you know, pertained to you because you had say so and you're not just sitting there, looking at your watch hoping it'll be time to go home. In the teacher culture circle, we often were surprised by how late it was when we finally had time to look at our watches.

Effects on Teachers' Beliefs and Practices

In the struggle between saying and doing in which we must engage to diminish the distance between them, it is just as possible to change what is said to make it fit the doing as it is to change the doing to make it fit what is said. This is why consistency ends up forcing a new choice. In the moment that I discover the inconsistency between what I say and what I do—progressive discourse, authoritarian practice—if, reflecting, at times painfully, I learn the ambiguity in which I find myself, I feel I am not able to continue like this and I look for a way out. In this way, a new choice is imposed on me. Either I change the progressive discourse for a discourse consistent with my reactionary practice, or I change my practice for a democratic one, adapting it to the progressivist discourse. (Freire, 1998, pp. 67-68)

Hillary: I mean it really made you think you really had to be reflective in it. So the process, being reflective then, trying to really put into practice things that we were talking about in the study group, kept us honest.

Lexy: From the very beginning it was SO educational and so interesting, and so just down-to-earth and personable, you know. We were all just discussing and, I mean, I just learned SO MUCH. But when we left, we put those plans to action, and we supported each other, and we held each other accountable. We also started helping our kids learn from each other using that same circle idea. We also saw how very important it is to be part of a group, of a community for learning. Coming together and learning from each other was amazing. You know, we have a teacher downstairs that's been teaching for fifteen, twenty years. We have a teacher teaching downstairs that knows a whole bunch of drama, has a Master's in drama. Using each other as resources, talking about what we had to offer was super neat.

Jill: I was able to take things that we talked about, strategies and solutions we talked about, and I feel like I was able to apply them in my classroom. So, it wasn't all about talk. It was talk and action.

Lexy: We listened and learned different ways to deal with particular situations. You get a totally different perspective from somebody else, and you can look at your problems or your stresses in a different way. So, if you're stressed out, you know, if you are part of a group, of a community, that others feel the same way. When you ask, it's like, oh my gosh, absolutely. Then, at least you know that you are not, like, totally incompetent.

((Many teachers agreed))

Marilyn: Mariana had talked about, like, doing a gallery walk. She had seen something like that in a public school in New York City, to communicate what's going on in classrooms, and we all get to preview and talk about it. Then parents could come in and talk and see what's going on in the classrooms, 'cause like, sometimes the parents really are unsure what's going on in the classrooms.

Lexy: We thought it was a good idea, but we decided to put together a brochure that talked about what were some of the core ideas that guided our teaching and decisions in the classroom. So, the teacher culture circles influenced our teaching and the way we communicated with parents.

James: But I think one of the things we did not address well is the fact that everyone, the parents, they read it individually, they're not there experiencing it together. I think that, of course, what I learned from the teacher study group, is that we all experienced it together, and that, I think was what made the difference.

Marilyn: ((keeps nodding)) It was just that amazing!

James: The teacher culture circles were grounded on a vision of change, which is an on-going process. That's what we're talking about here. If an issue is not addressed, it's gonna come back up again, or it can come back up next week. It's all on the table. There was no illusion that everything was going to be alright and that every problem was going to have a satisfactory solution within a period of time, like two or three hours. Besides dealing with everyday issues, this influenced my philosophy and approach to teaching.

Marilyn: Right, and just getting feedback on what you're doing in the classroom, which is huge. Thinking about what is and hoping for what is going to be, and taking this approach with our students, helping them think and question as they grow.

James: Yes, yes, it is so important, it is so important!

Corry: As a teacher, I can say that the effect of our teacher culture circles on me was to de-stress and think of ways to deal with issues on smaller and larger levels. Before, I would be in the classroom, you know, and it's easy to think, oh, I am the only one going through this, or our class is the only one going through this, or our kids are the only ones doing this. There was a community that allowed me to recognize the stresses of teaching as a process rather than personal punishment. Every time after we had a meeting, I felt I came away from there, like, either feeling like validated or, helped in some way, or that I helped someone. So, that, that, just that overall general feeling is what I think kept me wanting to be back, the empowering process that made me believe I can do this.

James: I love teacher study group. It did kind of fire up my teaching. I started seeing how kids could ask questions and be critical too and how they had the power to change things. It inspired me to try new things because I knew I could try something and go to teacher culture circle and say, ooh, I tried this and this worked, and that didn't work and we could problem solve together. Because I think if you just continue teaching in the same way over and over again, day and month, and year out, then you just become dull, you can be just like a slump, and, and you become a tired teacher.

Many Voices, Multiple Perspectives

My ethical duty, as one of the subjects, one of the agents, of a practice that can never be neutral—the educational—is to express my respect for differences in ideas and positions. I must respect even positions opposed to my own, positions that I combat earnestly and with passion. (Freire, 2004, p. 66)

Mollie: It was participant directed. A traditional seminar might be helpful if it's about topics that you're unfamiliar with, and somebody that's really knowledgeable in the area comes in and talks about their specialty. But all you do is listen and take it in. There is no connection between theory and practice. It's up to you. In the teacher culture circle, we theorized from our practices, together. We really directed the conversation. It wasn't like one person speaking to all of us and us responding, it was all of us responding to one another. There was respect of difference and I think this is why it worked.

Jill: I found out, I found very quickly, all of us're very DIFFERENT too. I mean we're kind o' like all working toward the same goal, but we're doing it in different ways. We have different personalities, and just brought a lot to the group.

Hillary: Yea. There were some instances where we might disagree or we might talk about subjects that might be uncomfortable for a lot of people. It DIDN'T happen all the time, and when it did, it was dealt with respect.

Shante: In those times, Mariana was very good at keeping our focus, bringing it back to the issue. Sometimes, we realized that we tended to avoid conflict. But we learned that even though many of us had grown up thinking that conflict was bad, it was a place where we learned.

Marilyn: So, she [the facilitator] asked us to keep bringing perspectives we were good at, listening, saying okay I hear what

your concerns are, you know, but just bringing back the focus of what we were discussing. So, the facilitator, was
kinda, was important for all voices to be heard.

Jill: Yes, I definitely think so,

Corry: But we had to keep reminding ourselves that many voices,
opinions, experiences are part of what make a community so
important, so we could learn from other teachers.

Lexy: ((nods))

An Invitation

These teachers' voices illustrate how "A world may come into being
in the course of a continuing dialogue" (Greene, 1995, p. 196). I sincerely hope that this book inspires you to embrace Freire's critical,
hopeful, and liberatory pedagogy. I hope that you come to realize the
possibilities afforded by Freirean culture circles across contexts. After
all, "we who believe in freedom cannot rest until it's done" (Ayers,
1989, p. 520).

Afterword

by William Ayers

University of Illinois at Chicago

In 1963 Charlie Cobb, then a student at Howard University, wrote a brief proposal for a Summer Freedom School designed to reenergize and refocus the Civil Rights Movement in Mississippi. Cobb claimed that while the Black children in the South were denied many things—decent school facilities, honest and forward-looking curricula, fully qualified teachers—the fundamental injury was "a complete absence of academic freedom, and students are forced to live in an environment that is geared to squashing intellectual curiosity, and different thinking." He called the classrooms of Mississippi "intellectual wastelands," and he challenged himself and others "to fill an intellectual and creative vacuum in the lives of young Negro Mississippi, and to get them to articulate their own desires, demands and questions." Their own desires, their own demands, their own questions—for African Americans living in semifeudal bondage, managed and contained through a system of law and custom as well as outright terror, this was beyond imagination.

Cobb was crossing hard lines of propriety and tradition, convention and common sense, and he knew it. He was poised to break the law and overthrow a system, and his modest proposal was designed to challenge the taken-for-granted, shake the settled, and plow a deep and promising furrow toward freedom and the unknown. It was insurrection itself.

Cobb's vision came to life in 1964 with the launching of Freedom Schools throughout the South and the publication of the Mississippi Freedom School Curriculum, a document shaped not by the articulation of content to be transmitted, but by an escalating set of questions to investigate and explore. That same year a U.S.-backed military coup overthrew the popular government of Brazil, and Paulo Freire, a young educator recently appointed to direct the Brazilian National Literacy Program, was arrested, jailed, and eventually exiled. Freire had become widely known for his work developing something he called "culture circles," sites of literacy learning based on the idea that in order for education to realize its transformative and liberating potential, people would need to find ways to *articulate their own desires, demands, and questions.*

In both Paulo Freire's work and in the work of the Freedom Schools people were invited to affirm their own humanity and experiences and to build their learning, growth, and action projects on the rock of their own strengths, their own wisdom: "If we are concerned with breaking the power structure," Cobb wrote, "then we have to be concerned with building up our own institutions to replace the old, unjust, decadent ones..." "Students," Freire argued, "as they are increasingly posed with problems relating to themselves in the world and with the world, will feel increasingly challenged and obliged to respond to that challenge." Coming from different corners of the world (and unaware of one another), grappling with issues of oppression and exploitation, each invented an effective educational intervention that articulated a radical critique of an unjust social order and demanded fundamental change. Both drew on the experiences and knowledge of the downtrodden themselves, arguing that the people with the problems are also necessarily the people with the solutions, and both enacted on the ground a vision of participatory democracy and simple justice. People named a world that could be but is not yet; they organized themselves to live against the grain, against unnecessary suffering and undeserved pain; and everyone struggled to live *in search of* rather than *in accordance with* or *in accommodation to* the given world.

Freire, Teaching, and Learning: Culture Circles across Contexts deepens and extends the natural history of what we sometimes call critical or liberatory teaching, the pedagogy most often identified with Paulo Freire, but not unique to Brazil, to adult education, or to literacy. Mariana Souto-Manning's accomplishment is to show us just how varied and widespread, how close at hand, the practice of teaching for freedom can be. This wild voyage of discovery and surprise illuminates a rich and varied landscape of possibility, a landscape to nourish our humanistic aspirations as teachers.

Those aspirations push us toward the direct and unequivocal link between critical pedagogy and democracy. All schools serve the societies in which they're embedded—authoritarian schools serve authoritarian systems, apartheid schools serve apartheid society, and so on. Practically all educators want their students to study hard, stay away from drugs, do their homework, and learn the subject matters. In fact none of these features distinguishes schools in the old Soviet Union or fascist Germany or medieval Saudi Arabia from schools in a democracy, and indeed those schools produced some excellent scientists and athletes and musicians and generals. They also produced obedience and conformity, moral blindness and easy agreement, obtuse patriotism and a willingness to follow orders right into the furnaces.

In a democracy one would expect something different and something more—a commitment to free inquiry, questioning, and participation; a push for access and equity; a curriculum that encourages independent thought and singular judgment; a standard of full recognition of the humanity of each individual. At its heart, schools in a democracy would foreground and embrace the principle that the full development of each is necessary for the full development of all, and conversely, that the full development of all is the condition for the full development of each.

There is a more fundamental purpose to schooling in a democracy—at least theoretically—than either loyalty to the state or fealty to the leaders or job training: people in a free society must know how to think about the issues that affect their lives and how they might act to change things. Pressure from government to make schools little outposts of patriotism and military recruitment, or from business to make the goals of education identical to the needs of corporations, jeopardizes the democratic foundations of education. We must ask ourselves whether schools geared to preparing loyal subjects or obedient workers also build thinking, literate, active, fully developed and morally sensitive citizens who carry out their democratic responsibilities to one another, to their communities, to the earth.

Teaching for obedience and conformity is characterized by authoritarianism and irrelevance, passivity and fatalism. It turns on the little technologies for control and normalization—the elaborate schemes for managing the crowd; the knotted system of rules and discipline; the exhaustive machinery of schedules and clocks; the laborious programs of testing and grading, assessment, judgment, and evaluation—all of it adding up to a familiar cave, an intricately constructed hierarchy with everyone in a designated place and a place for every one. Knowing and accepting one's pigeonhole on the vast and barren mountainside becomes the entire lesson.

Participatory democracy by contrast insists that the people themselves must decide, and at its heart it generates and requires dialogue—each one speaking with the hope of being heard, each one listening with the possibility of being changed.

Teachers today, as teachers in all times and all places, must decide whether to be dutiful clerks inculcating into students the status quo, the social order as it is, obediently passing along the received curriculum that's been handed to them, or to move beyond sorting and shaping, striking out in pursuit of the new, questioning and challenging all that is before them, anything that strikes their infinite curiosity or offends their deepest values. Teachers have to ask themselves whether they're up for being bold and taking risks.

We begin by engaging a fundamental question, sometimes explicitly, often not: Who in the world am I? Who am I in the world? And from this: What are my choices? What are my chances? What will I do to make my way through? The thoughtful teacher, the ethical teacher, the critical and liberatory teacher, takes the questions as challenge and mandate.

"Insane generosity," Albert Camus writes in *The Rebel* "is the generosity of rebellion." It may be that man is mortal, he said, "but let us die resisting; and if our lot is complete annihilation, let us not behave in such a way that it seems justice!" Camus speaks of a generosity that consistently refuses injustice, that is determined to allow nothing to pass, and that makes no calculations as to what it offers. "Real generosity toward the future," Camus concludes, "lies in giving all to the present." Giving it all, here and now, the only time we've got. This is the watchword for teachers who embrace the core values of teaching in and for democracy, and trudging toward freedom.

References

Alexander, B., Anderson, G. L., & Gallegos, B. (Eds.). (2005). *Performance theory and education: Power, pedagogy, and the politics of identity*. Mahwah, NJ: LEA.

Allen, J. (2007). *Creating welcoming schools: A practical guide to home-school partnerships with diverse families*. New York: Teachers College Press.

Anderson, G. T. (2005). Innovations in early childhood teacher education: Reflections on practice. *Journal of Early Childhood Teacher Education, 26*(1), 91-95.

Anderson, G., & Irvine, J. (1993). Informing critical literacy with ethnography. In C. Lankshear and P. McLaren (Eds.), *Critical literacy: Politics, praxis, and the postmodern*. Albany: State University of New York Press.

Andrews, J., Carnine, D., Coutinho, M., Edgar, E., Forness, S., Fuchs, L., Jordan, D., Kauffman, J., Patton, J., Paul, J., Rosell, J., Rueda, R., Schiller, E., Skrtic, T., & Wong, J. (2000). Bridging the special education divide. *Remedial and Special Education, 21*(5), 258-260.

Apple, M., Gandin, L., & Hypolito, A. (2001). Paulo Freire, 1921-97. In J. Palmer (Ed.). *Fifty modern thinkers on education: From Piaget to the present day*. London: Routledge.

Araújo, V. C. (1991). *Democratização, educação e cidadania: Caminho do Governo Arraes*. São Paulo, Brazil: Cortez.

Archer, M. (2003). *Structure, agency and the internal conversation*. Cambridge: Cambridge University Press.

Aronson, J., Harré, R., & Way, E. (1995). *Realism rescued: How scientific progress is possible*. London: Duckworth.

Ayers, W. (2004). *Teaching toward freedom: Moral commitment and ethical action in the classroom*. Boston, MA: Beacon Press.

Ayers, W. C. (2001). *To teach: The journey of a teacher*, 2nd edition. New York: Teachers College Press.

Ayers, W. C. (1989). "We who believe in freedom cannot rest until it's done": Two dauntless women of the civil rights movement and the education of a people. *Harvard Educational Review, 59*(4), 520-528.

Azevedo, C., Domeneci, T., Amaral, M., Tendler, S., Viana, N., Arbex J., Jr., et al. (2004). O golpe de 64. *Caros Amigos Especial, 19*.

Babbage, F. (2004). *Augusto Boal*. New York: Routledge.

Bahruth, R., & Steiner, S. (2000). Upstream in the mainstream: Pedagogy against the current. In S. Steiner, H. M. Krank, P. McLaren, and R. Bahruth (Eds.), *Freirean pedagogy, praxis, and possibilities: Projects for the new millennium* (pp. 119-146). New York: Falmer Press.

Banks, J. (2007). Series foreword. In C. D. Lee (Ed.), *Culture, literacy, and learning* (pp. xi-xv). New York: Teachers College Press.

Banks, J. A. (1995). Multicultural education and curriculum transformation. *Journal of Negro Education*, 64(4), 390.

Banks, J. A. (2004). Multicultural education: Historical development, dimensions, and practice. In J. A. Banks & C. A. Banks (Eds.), *Handbook of research on multicultural education* (2nd ed.) (pp. 3-29), San Francisco, CA: Jossey Bass.

Banks, J., & Banks, C. A. M. (Eds.). (2004). *Multicultural education: Issues and perspectives* (5th ed.). Hoboken, NJ: John Wiley.

Bartolomé, L. I. (1996). Beyond the methods fetish: Toward a humanizing pedagogy. In P. Leistyna, A. Woodrum, & S. A. Sherblom (Eds.), *Breaking free: The transformative power of critical pedagogy* (pp. 229-252). Cambridge, MA: Harvard Graduate School of Education.

Bee, B. (1980). The politics of literacy. In R. Mackie (Ed.), *Literacy and revolution: The pedagogy of Paulo Freire*. London: Pluto Press.

Behar, R. (1996). *The vulnerable observer: Anthropology that breaks your heart*. Boston: Beacon.

Berk, L. E., & Winsler, A. (1995). *Scaffolding children's learning: Vygotsky and early childhood education*. Washington, DC: National Association for the Education of Young Children.

Boal, A. (1974). *Teatro del oprimido y otras poeticas politicas*. Buenos Aires, Argentina: Ediciones de la Flor.

Boal, A. (1979). *Theatre of the oppressed*. London: Pluto Press.

Boal, A. (1995). *Rainbow of desire: The Boal method of theatre and therapy* (trans. A. Jackson). London: Routledge.

Boal, A. (2000). *Theater of the oppressed* (new edition). London, UK: Pluto Press.

Boal, A. (2005). *Democracy now: The war and peace report*. Retrieved May 3, 2009 from: http://www.democracynow.org/2005/6/3/famed_brazilian_artist_augusto_boal_on

Bowers, C. A. (1987). *Elements of a post-liberal theory of education*. New York: Teachers College Press.

Boxer, M. J. (1998). *When women ask the questions: Creating women's studies in America*. Baltimore, MD: Johns Hopkins University Press.

Brandão, C. (2001). *De Angicos a ausentes: 40 anos de educação popular*. Porto Alegre, Brazil: MOVA-RS.

Bredekamp, S., & Copple, C. (2009). *Developmentally appropriate practice in early childhood programs* (3rd. ed.). Washington, DC: National Association for the Education of Young Children (NAEYC).

Breton, M. (1995). The potential for social action in groups. *Social Work in Groups*, 18(2/3), 5-13.

Brown, C. (1975). *Literacy in 30 hours*. London: Readers and Writers Co-op.

Brown, C. (1978). *Literacy in 30 hours: Paulo Freire's process in northeast Brazil*. Chicago: Alternate Schools Network.

Cahnmann, M., Rymes, B., & Souto-Manning, M. (2005). Using critical discourse analysis to understand and facilitate identification processes of bilingual adults becoming teachers. *Critical Inquiry in Language Studies: An International Journal*, 2(4), 195-213.

Cahnmann-Taylor, M., & Souto-Manning, M. (2010). *Teachers act up!* New York: Teachers College Press.

Cahnmann-Taylor, M., Wooten, J., Souto-Manning, M., & Dice, J. (2009, in press). The art & science of educational inquiry: Analysis of performance-based focus groups with novice bilingual teachers. *Teachers College Record*.

Cannella, G. S., & Reiff, J. C. (1994). Individual constructivist teacher education: Teachers as empowered learners. *Teacher Education Quarterly*, 21(3), 27-38.

Carger, C. L. (1996). *Of borders and dreams: A Mexican-American experience of urban education*. New York: Teachers College Press.

Carter, R., & Goodwin, A. L. (1994). Racial identity and education. *Review of Research in Education*, 20, 291-336.

Cazden, C. (1986). Classroom discourse. In M. C. Wittrock (Ed.), *Handbook of research on teaching* (Vol. 3, pp. 432–463). New York: Macmillan.

Chouliaraki, L., & Fairclough, N. (1999). *Discourse in late modernity*. Edinburgh: Edinburgh University Press.

Coben, D. (1998). *Radical heroes: Gramsci, Freire and the politics of adult education*. New York: Garland.

Cochran-Smith, M., & Fries, M. K. (2001). Sticks, stones, and ideology: The discourse of reform in teacher education. *Educational Researcher*, 30(8), 3–15.

Cochran-Smith, M., & Lytle, S. L. (1990). Research on teaching and teacher research: The issues that divide. *Educational Researcher*, 19(2), 2-11.

Codron, D. (2007). Stratification and educational sorting: Explaining ascriptive inequalities in childhood reading group placement. *Social problems*, 54(1), pp. 139-160.

Coleman, E. (1996). *White socks only*. Morton Grove, IL: Albert Whitman & Company.

Coles, R. (1995). *The story of Ruby Bridges*. New York: Scholastic.

Comber, B. (2003). Critical literacy in the early years: What does it look like? In N. Hall, J. Larson, and J. Marsh (Eds.), *Handbook of early childhood literacy*. London, UK: Sage.

Coutinho, M. J., & Oswald, D. P. (2000). Disproportionate representation in special education: A synthesis and recommendations. *Journal of Child and Family Studies*, 9(2), 135-152.

Cowhey, M. (2006, November). *Thinking critically and teaching differently in the primary grades*. Paper presented at the Annual National Council of Teacher of English Convention. Nashville, TN.

Cummins, J., & Sayers, D. (1995). *Brave new schools: challenging cultural illiteracy through global learning networks*. New York: St. Martin's Press.

Darder, A. (2002). *Reinventing Paulo Freire: A pedagogy of love*. Boulder, CO: Westview Press.

Darling-Hammond, L. (2000). How teacher education matters. *Journal of Teacher Education*, 51(3), 166-173.

Darling-Hammond, L. (2006). Foreword. In C. D. Lee (2007), *Culture, literacy, and learning: Taking bloom in the midst of the whirlwind* (pp. xvii-xxii). New York: Teachers College Press.

de Castro, J. (1969). *Death in the North-East*. New York: Vintage.

de Figueiredo-Cowen, M. and Gastaldo, D. (1995). *Paulo Freire at the institute*. London: Institute of Education, University of London.

Delpit, L. (1988). The silenced dialogue: Power and pedagogy in educating other people's children. *Harvard Educational Review*, 58(3) 280-298.

Delpit, L. (1995). *Other people's children: Cultural conflict in the classroom*. New York: The New Press.

Delpit, L. (1998). Ebonics and culturally responsive instruction. In T. Perry and L. Delpit (Eds.), *The real Ebonics debate: Power, language, and the education of African-American children*. Boston: Beacon Press.

Dewey, J. (1897). My pedagogic creed. *The School Journal*, 54(3), 77-80.

Dyson, A. H. (1999). Transforming transfer: Unruly children, contrary texts, and the persistence of the pedagogical order. In A. Iran-Nejad and D. Pearson (Eds.), *Review of research in education: Volume 24*. Washington, DC: American Educational Research Association..

Dyson, A. H. (2008). On listening to child composers: Beyond "fix-its." In C. Genishi & A. L. Goodwin (Eds.), *Diversities in early childhood education: Rethinking and doing* (pp. 13-28). New York: Routledge.

Dyson, A. H., & Genishi, C. (2005). *On the case: Approaches to language and literacy research*. New York: Teachers College Press.

Edmond, G., & Tilley, E. (2007). Beyond role play: Workplace theatre and employee relations. Retrieved October 16, 2007, from http://praxis.massey.ac.nz/fileadmin/praxis/papers/GEdmondETilleyPaper_20.pdf

Elias, J. (1994). *Paulo Freire: Pedagogue of revolution*. Malibar, FL: Krieger.

Ellsworth, E. (1992). Why doesn't this feel empowering? Working through the repressive myths of critical pedagogy. In C. Luke & J. Gore (Eds.), *Feminisms and critical pedagogy*. New York: Routledge.

Fairclough, N. (2003). *Analysing discourse: Textual analysis for social research*. London: Routledge.

Fairclough, N. (2004). Semiotic aspects of social transformation and learning. In R. Rogers (Ed.), *An introduction to critical discourse analysis in education*. Mahwah, NJ: Lawrence Erlbaum Associates.

Fecho, B. (2004). *"Is this English?" Race, language, and culture in the classroom*. New York: Teachers' College Press.

Feitosa, S. (1999a). Paulo Freire e o social construtivismo. In A. Yamasaki, E. Santos, L. do Nascimento, & S. Feitosa, *Cadernos de EJA 2: Educação de jovens e adultos, uma perspective freireana*. São Paulo, Brazil: Instituto Paulo Freire.

Feitosa, S. (1999b). *Método Paulo Freire: Princípios e práticas de uma concepção popular de educação*. Unpublished master's thesis. Universidade de São Paulo, São Paulo, Brazil.

Fennimore, B. S. (2000). *Talk matters: Refocusing the language of public schooling*. New York: Teachers College Press.

Fennimore, B. S. (2008). Talk about children: Developing a living curriculum of advocacy and social justice. In C. Genishi & A. L. Goodwin (Eds.), *Diversities in early childhood education: Rethinking and doing* (pp. 185-199). New York: Teachers College Press.

Finger, M., & Asún, J. M. (2001). *Adult education and the crossroads*. New York: Palgrave.

Fraser, N. (1997). *Justice interruptus: Critical reflections on the "postsocialist" condition*. New York & London: Routledge.

Freire, P. (1959). *Educação e atualidade brasileira*. Unpublished doctoral dissertation. Universidade de Recife, Recife, Brazil.

Freire, P. (1967). *Educação como prática da liberdade*. Rio de Janeiro: Paz e Terra.

Freire, P. (1970). *Pedagogy of the oppressed*. New York: Continuum.

Freire, P. (1971). Conscientisation-Unveiling and transforming reality. In C. Wright (Ed.), *Education for liberation and community* (pp. 3-6). Melbourne, Australia: Australian Council of Churches.

Freire, P. (1974/1976). *Education: The practice of freedom*. London: Writers and Readers.

Freire, P. (1978). *Pedagogy in process: The letters to Guinea-Bissau*. New York: Seabury Press.

Freire, P. (1982). *Sobre educação (diálogos), Volume 1*. Rio de Janeiro: Paz e Terra.

Freire, P. (1985). *The politics of education: Culture, power, and liberation*. Westport, CT: Bergin & Garvin.

Freire, P. (1987). Letter to North-American teachers (C. Hunter, Trans.). In I. Shor (Ed.), *Freire for the classroom: A source book for liberatory teaching*. Portsmouth, NH: Heinemann.

Freire, P. (1990). *Education for critical consciousness*. South Hadley, MA: Bergin & Garvey.

Freire, P. (1992). *Pedagogia da esperança: Um reencontro com a pedagogia do oprimido*. Rio de Janeiro: Paz e Terra.

Freire, P. (1995). *À sombra desta mangueira*. São Paulo: Olho d'água.

Freire, P. (1996). *Letters to Cristina* (D. Macedo, Trans.). New York & London: Routledge.

Freire, P. (1997). *Pedagogy of the oppressed*. New York: Continuum.

Freire, P. (1998). *Teachers as cultural workers: Letters to those who dare teach*. Oxford: Westview Press.

Freire, P. (2000). *Pedagogy of the oppressed* (30th anniversary ed.). New York: Continuum.

Freire, P. (2004). *Pedagogy of hope.* New York: Continuum.

Freire, P., & Macedo, D. (1987). *Literacy: Reading the word and the world.* Westport, CT: Bergin & Garvey.

Freire, P., & Macedo, D. (1989). *Literacy: Reading the word and the world.* South Hadley, MA: Bergin & Harvey.

Freire, P., & Macedo, D. (1995). A dialogue: Culture, language, and race. *Harvard Educational Review,* 65(3), 377-402.

Gadotti, M. & Romão, J. (2002). *Educação de jovens e adultos: Teoria, prática e proposta.* São Paulo, Brazil: Cortez/Instituto Paulo Freire.

Gadotti, M. (1994). *Reading Paulo Freire: His life and work.* Albany: State University of New York Press.

Galdone, P. (1970). *The three little pigs.* New York: Clarion Books.

Gay, G. (1995). Mirror images on common issues: Parallels between multicultural education and critical pedagogy. In C. E. Sleeter and P. McLaren (Eds.), *Multicultural education, critical pedagogy, and the politics of difference* (pp. 155-190). Albany: State University of New York Press.

Gay, G. (2004). Beyond brown: Promoting equality through multicultural education. *Journal of Curriculum and Supervision,* 19, 193–217.

Gee, J. P. (1996). *Social linguistics and literacies: Ideology in discourse.* London: Taylor & Francis.

Gee, J. P. (2001). Identity as an analytic lens for research in education. *Review of Research in Education* 25, 99-125.

Genishi, C., & Dyson, A. H. (2009). *Children, language, and literacy: Diverse learners in diverse times.* New York: Teachers College Press.

Genishi, C., & Goodwin, A. L. (Eds.). (2008). *Diversities in early childhood education: Rethinking and doing.* New York: Routledge.

Gerhardt, H. (1993). Paulo Freire (1921-), *Prospects,* 21(87/88), 439-58.

Getzel, G. S. (2003). Group work and social justice: Rhetoric or action? In Association for the Advancement of Social Work with Groups (Ed.), *Social work with groups: Social justice through personal, community, and societal change.* Binghamton, NY: The Haworth Press.

Gillborn, D. (2005). Education policy as an act of White supremacy: Whiteness, critical race theory and education reform. *Journal of Educational Policy,* 20(4), 485-505.

Gillborn, D. (2006). Critical race theory and education: Racism and anti-racism in educational theory and praxis. *Discourse Studies in the Cultural Politics of Education,* 27(1), 11-32.

Giroux, H. (1985). Introduction. In P. Freire, *The politics of education: Culture, power, and liberation* (pp. xi-xxvi). Westport, CT: Bergin & Garvin.

Giroux, H. (1987). Introduction. In P. Freire & D. Macedo, *Literacy: Reading the word and the world.* Westport, CT: Bergin & Garvey.

Giroux, H. (1997). *Pedagogy and the politics of hope: Theory, culture, and schooling.* Boulder, CO: Westview.

Gomez, M. L., & Abt-Perkins, D. (1995). Sharing Stories of Teaching for Practice, Analysis, and Critique. *Education Research and Perspectives,* 22(1), 39-52.

Gomez, M. L. (2002). The role of talk in learning to teach. *Curriculum and Teaching,* 17(2), 37-53.

Goodwin, A. L., Cheruvu, R., & Genishi, C. (2008). Responding to multiple diversities in early childhood education: How far have we come? In C. Genishi and A. L. Goodwin (Eds.), *Diversities in early childhood: Rethinking and doing* (pp. 3-10). New York: Routledge.

Gore, J. (1993). *The struggle for pedagogies: Critical and feminist discourses as regimes of truth.* New York: Routledge.

Goulet, D. (2005). Introduction. In P. Freire, *Education for critical consciousness* (pp. vii-xiii). New York: Continuum.

Grant, C., & Sleeter, C. (1996). *After the school bell rings.* Bristol, PA: Falmer Press.

Graue, M. E. (2006). The answer is readiness, now what is the question? *Early Education & Development,* 17(1), pp. 43-56.

Greene, M. (1995). *Releasing the imagination: Essays on education, the arts, and social change.* San Francisco: Jossey-Bass.

Gregory, E., Long, S., & Volk, D. (Eds.). (2004). *Many pathways to literacy: Young children learning with siblings, grandparents, peers and communities.* New York and London: RoutledgeFalmer.

Gutiérrez, K. D. (2008). Developing a sociocritical literacy in the third space. *Reading Research Quarterly,* 43(2), 148–164.

Gutierrez, L., and Lewis, E. (1998). A feminist perspective on organizing with women of color. In F. Rivera and J. Erlich (Eds.), *Community organizing in a diverse society* (Third edition) (pp. 97-106). Boston: Allyn & Bacon.

Habermas, (1987). *The theory of communicative action vol. 2, Lifeworld and system: A critique of functionalist reason.* London: Heinemann.

Haddad, S., & Freitas, M. (1991). *Diagnóstico dos estudos e pesquisas.* Brasília, Brazil: MEC – Ministério de Educação e Cultura.

Harding, S. (1986). *The science question in feminism.* Ithaca, NY: Cornell University Press.

Harste, J., Breau, A., Leland, C., Lewison, M., Ociepka, A., & Vasquez, V. (2000). Supporting critical conversations. In K. M. Pierce (Ed.), *Adventuring with books.* Urbana, IL: National Council of Teachers of English.

Heaney, T. (1989). *Issues in Freirean pedagogy.* Retrieved January 15, 2000 from http://nlu.nl.edu/ace/Resources/Documents/FreireIssues.html

Heath, S. B. (1983). *Ways with words: Language, life, and work in communities and classrooms.* New York: Cambridge University Press.

Hill Collins, P. (1990). *Black feminist thought: Knowledge, consciousness, and the politics of empowerment.* Boston: Unwin Hyman.

Hill Collins, P. (2000). *Black feminist thought: Knowledge, consciousness, and the politics of empowerment* (2nd ed.). New York: Routledge.

Hill, L. T., Stremmel, A. J., & Fu, V. R. (2004). *Teaching as inquiry: Rethinking curriculum in early childhood education.* Boston: Allyn & Bacon.

Hoffman, D. M. (1996). Culture and self in multicultural education: Reflections on discourse, text, and practice. *American Educational Research Journal, 33*(3), 545-569.

Holland, D., Skinner, D., & Cain, C. (2001). *Identity and agency in cultural worlds.* Cambridge, MA: Harvard University Press.

hooks, b. (1990). *Yearning: Race, gender, and cultural politics.* Boston: South End Press.

hooks, b. (1994). *Teaching to transgress.* New York: Routledge.

Horton, M., & Freire, P. (1990). *We make the road by walking: Conversations on education and social change.* Philadelphia, PA: Temple University Press.

Howard, L. A. (2004). Speaking theatre/Doing pedagogy: Re-visiting "theatre of the oppressed." *Communication Education, 53,* 217-233.

Huber, T., Kune, F. M., Bakkem, L., & Clark, F. L. (1997). Transforming teacher education: Including culturally responsible pedagogy. In J. King, E. R. Hollins, and W. C. Hayman (Eds.), *Preparing teachers for cultural diversity.* New York: Teachers College Press.

Huerta-Macias, A. (1993). *Current terms in adult ESL literacy.* Washington, DC: National Clearinghouse on Literacy Education.

Hughes, E. (1999). "If you have sun and you have rain you get a rainbow": Creating meaningful curriculum. *Journal of Early Childhood Teacher Education, 20,* 89-100.

Hull, G., & Schultz, K. (Eds.). (2002). *School's out! Bridging out-of-school literacies with classroom practice.* New York: Teachers College Press.

Instituto Paulo Freire (n.d.). *Instituto Paulo Freire.* São Paulo, Brazil: Insituto Paulo Freire.

Instituto Paulo Freire. (Producer), Gadotti, M., & Antunes, A. (Directors). (n.d.). *Paulo Freire: Coleção grandes educadores.* [Motion picture]. (Available from ATTA Mídia e Educação, Rua Ministro Sinesio Rocha, 209, São Paulo, São Paulo, Brazil).

James, T. (1980). *Can the mountains speak for themselves?* Retrieved May 31, 2009 from http://wilderdom.com/facilitation/Mountains.html

Janks, H. (2000). Domination, access, diversity and design: A synthesis for critical literacy education. *Educational Review, 52*(2), 175-186.

Jensen, M. (1999). Developing pedagogical knowledge through teacher-written case stories. *Journal of Early Childhood Teacher Education, 20,* 181-184.

Johansson, J. (2006). Will there be any preschool teachers in the future? A comment on recent teacher-education reforms. In J. Einarsdottir & J. T. Wagner (Eds.), *Nordic childhoods and early education* (pp. 43-69). Charlotte, NC: Information Age Publishing (IAP).

Katz, L. F., & Woodin, E. M. (2002). Hostility, hostile detachment, and conflict engagement in marriages: Effects on child and family functioning. *Child development, 73*(2), 636-651.

Keesing-Styles, L. (2003). The relationship between critical pedagogy and assessment in teacher education. *Radical Pedagogy*, 5(1), 1-20.

Kincheloe, J. (2005). *Critical pedagogy*. New York: Peter Lang.

Kincheloe, J., & McLaren, P. (2005). Rethinking critical theory and qualitative research. In N. Denzin & Y. Lincoln (Eds.), *The Sage handbook of qualitative research* (3rd ed., pp. 303-342). London: Sage.

Kincheloe, J., & Steinberg, S. (1998). Lesson plans from the outer limits: Unauthorized methods. In J. Kincheloe & S. Steinberg (Eds.), *Unauthorized methods: Strategies for critical teaching* (pp. 1-23). New York: Routledge.

Kincheloe, J., Steinberg, S., Rodriguez, N., & Chennault, R. (1998). *White reign: Deploying Whiteness in America*. New York: St. Martin's Press.

Ladson-Billings, G. (1994). *The dreamkeepers: Successful teachers of African American children*. San Francisco: Jossey-Bass Publishers.

Ladson-Billings, G. (1996). Multicultural issues in the classroom: Race, class, and gender. In R. W. Evans and W. Saxe (Eds.), *Handbook on teaching social issues*. Washington DC: NCSS.

Ladson-Billings, G. (2004). Just what is critical race theory and what's it doing in a nice field like education. In G. Ladson-Billings and D. Gillborn (Eds.), *The RoutledgeFalmer reader in multicultural education*. London: RoutledgeFalmer.

Ladson-Billings, G., & Tate, W. (1995). Toward a critical race theory of education. *Teachers College Record*, 97(1), pp. 47-68.

Lee, J. (2002). Racial and ethnic achievement gap trends: Reversing the progress toward equity? *Educational Researcher*, 31(1), 3-12.

Lee, J. A. B. (1994). *The empowerment approach to social work practice*. New York: Columbia University Press.

Lewison, M., Seely Flint, A., & Van Sluys, K. (2002). Taking on critical literacy: The journey of newcomers and novices. *Language Arts*, 79(5), 382-392.

Louis, R. (2005). Performing English, performing bodies: A case for critical performative language pedagogy. *Text and Performance Quarterly*, 25(4), 334–353.

Lucas, S. R. (2001). Effectively maintained inequality: Education transitions, track mobility, and social background effects. *American Journal of Sociology*, 106, 1642-1690.

Macedo, D., & Freire, A. M. A. (1998). Foreword. In P. Freire, *Teachers as cultural workers: Letters to those who dare teach*. Boulder, CO: Westview Press.

Manlove, E. (1994). Conflict and ambiguity over work roles: The impact on child care worker burnout. *Early Education and Development*, 5(1), 41-55.

Marsh, C., & Willis, G. (1999). *Curriculum: Alternative approaches, ongoing issues*. Upper Saddle River, NJ: Prentice Hall.

Marshall, J. (1989). *The three little pigs*. New York: Puffin Books.

Marsiglia, F. F. (2003). Culturally grounded approaches to social justice through social work with groups. In Association for the Advancement of Social Work with Groups (Ed.), *Social work with groups: Social justice through personal, community, and societal change*. Binghamton, NY: The Haworth Press.

Marsiglia, F. F., & Zorita, P. (1996). Narratives as a means to support Latino/a students in higher education. *Reflections, 2*(1), 54-62.

Mashayekh, F. (1974). Freire, the man, his ideas and their implications. *Literary Discussion, 5*(1), 1-62.

Mayo, P. (1999). *Gramsci, Freire and adult education: Possibilities for transformative action.* London: Zed Books.

McKissack, P. C. (2001), *Goin' someplace special.* New York: Atheneum.

McLaren, P. (2000). Paulo Freire's pedagogy of possibility. In S. Steiner, H. Krank, P. McLaren, & R. Bahruth (Eds.), *Freirean pedagogy, praxis and possibilities: Projects for the new millennium.* New York & London: Falmer Press.

McNicoll, P. (2003). Current innovations in social work with groups to address issues of social justice. In Association for the Advancement of Social Work with Groups (Ed.), *Social work with groups: Social justice through personal, community, and societal change.* Binghamton, NY: The Haworth Press.

Mehan, H. (1996). *Constructing school success: The consequences of untracking low-achieving students.* New York: Cambridge University Press.

Moll, L., Amanti, C., Neff, D., & Gonzalez, N. (1992). Funds of knowledge for teaching: Using a qualitative approach to connect homes and classrooms. *Theory into Practice, 31,* 132-141.

Moore, J. R. (2001). *The story of Martin Luther King Jr.* Nashville, TN: Candy Cane Press.

Nieto, S. (1999*). The light in their eyes: Creating multicultural learning communities.* New York: Teachers College Press.

Nieto, S. (2000). Placing equity front and center: Some thoughts on transforming teacher education for a new century. *Journal of Teacher Education, 51*(3), 180-187.

Nieto, S. (2002). *Language, culture, and teaching: Critical perspectives for a new century.* Mahwah, NJ: Lawrence Erlbaum.

Nieto, S. (2003). *What keeps teachers going?* New York: Teachers College Press.

Nieto, S. (2005). *Why we teach.* New York: Teachers College Press.

Nieto, S. (2007). Foreword. In G. Campano (Ed.), *Immigrant students and literacy: Reading, writing, and remembering* (pp. xi-xii). New York: Teachers College Press.

Nolte, D. (1998). *Children learn what they live.* New York: Workman Publishing Company.

O'Brien, J. (2001a). Children reading critically: A local history. In B. Comber and A. Simpson (Eds.), *Negotiating critical literacies in classrooms.* Mahwah, NJ: Lawrence Erlbaum.

O'Brien, J. (2001b). "I knew that already": How children's books limit inquiry. In S. Boran and B. Comber (Eds.), *Critiquing whole language and classroom inquiry.* Urbana, IL: National Council of Teachers of English.

Ochs, E., & Capps, L. (2001). *Living narrative: Creating lives in everyday storytelling.* Cambridge, MA: Harvard University Press.

Ochs, E., Smith, R., & Taylor, C. (1996). Detective stories at dinnertime: Problem solving through co-narration. In C. Briggs (Ed.), *Disorderly discourse: Narrative, conflict, and inequality.* New York: Oxford University Press.

Paley, V. G. (1986). On listening to what the children say. *Harvard Educational Review*, 56(2), 122-131.

Paley, V. G. (2007). Goldilocks and her sister: An anecdotal guide to the doll corner. *Harvard Educational Review*, 77(2), 144-151.

Parmentier, R. (1994). *Signs in society: Studies in semiotic anthropology*. Bloomington: Indiana University Press.

Parsons, T. (1959). The school class as a social system: Some of its functions in American society. *Harvard Educational Review*, 29, 297-318.

Paterson, D. (2005). *A brief biography of Augusto Boal*. Retrieved May 31, 2009 from: http://www.ptoweb.org/boal.html

Pelandré, N. (2002). *Ensinar e aprender com Paulo Freire: 40 horas 40 anos depois*. São Paulo, Brazil: Cortez/Biblioteca Freireana.

Peters, M., & Lankshear, C. (1994). Education and hermeneutics: A Freirean interpretation. In P. McLaren and C. Lankshear (*Eds.*), *Politics of liberation: Paths from Freire* (pp. 173-192). London: Routledge.

Pineau, E. L. (2002). Critical performative pedagogy: Fleshing out the politics of liberatory education. In N. Stucky & C. Wimmer (Eds.), Teaching performance studies (pp. 41-54). Carbondale: Southern Illinois University Press.

Porfilio, B. J., & Yu, T. (2006). "Student as consumer": A critical narrative of the commercialization of teacher education. *Journal for Critical Education Policy Studies*, 4(1). Accessed February 22, 2007 from http://www.jceps.com/index.php?pageID=article&articleID=56

Purcell-Gates, V., & Waterman, R. (2000). *Now we read, we see, we speak: Portrait of literacy development in a Freirean-based adult class*. Mahwah, NJ: Lawrence Erlbaum.

Purcell-Gates, V. (1995). *Other people's words: The cycle of low literacy*. Cambridge, MA: Harvard University Press.

Rhedding-Jones, J. (2002). An undoing of documents and other texts: Towards a critical multiculturalism in early childhood education. *Contemporary Issues in Early Childhood*, 3(1), 90-116.

Ribeiro, V. (1997). *Educação de jovens e adultos: Proposta curricular para o 1º segmento do ensino fundamental*. São Paulo, Brazil: Ação Educativa.

Roberts, P. (2000). *Education, literacy, and humanization: Exploring the work of Paulo Freire*. Westport, CT: Bergin & Garvey.

Rogers, D., & Babinski, L. (2002). *From isolation to conversation: Supporting new teachers' development*. Albany: State University of New York Press.

Rogers, R., & Mosley, M. (2006). Racial literacy in a second-grade classroom: Critical race theory, Whiteness studies, and literacy research. *Reading Research Quarterly*, 41(4), 462-495.

Rogoff, B. (2003). *The cultural nature of human development*. New York: Oxford University Press.

Rosenblatt, L. (1978). *The reader, the text, the poem: The transactional theory of the literary work*. Carbondale: Southern Illinois University Press.

Rust, F. (1999). Learning lessons about diversity: a field experiences in the preparation of teachers. *Journal of Early Childhood Teacher Education, 20,* 175-179.

Rymes, B. (2001). *Conversational borderlands: Language and identity in an alternative urban high school.* New York: Teachers College Press.

Rymes, B. (2009). *Classroom discourse analysis: A tool for critical reflection.* Cresskill, NJ: Hampton Press.

Rymes, B., Cahnmann-Taylor, M., & Souto-Manning, M. (2008). Bilingual teachers' performances of power and conflict. *Teaching Education, 19*(2), 105-119.

Salvio, P. (1998). On using the literacy portfolio to prepare teachers for "willfull world traveling." In W. F. Pinar (Ed.), *Curriculum: Toward new identities.* New York: Garland.

Scieszka, J. (1996). *The true story of the 3 little pigs.* London, UK: Puffin Books.

Secretaria de Educação e Esportes, Governo do Estado de Pernambuco (Producer). (1997). *Círculos de educação e cultura.* [Motion picture]. (Available from TV VIVA, Rua de São Bento, 344, Olinda, Pernambuco, Brazil).

Senge, P. M., Cambron-McCabe, N., Lucas, T., Smith, B., Dutton, J., & Kleiner, A. (2000). *Schools that learn: A fifth discipline fieldbook for educators, parents, and everyone who cares about education.* New York: Doubleday.

Shapiro, B. Z. (2003). Social justice and social work with groups: Fragile—handle with care. In Association for the Advancement of Social Work with Groups (Ed.), *Social work with groups: Social justice through personal, community, and societal change.* Binghamton, NY: The Haworth Press.

Shaull, R. (2000). Foreword. In P. Freire, *Pedagogy of the oppressed* (pp. 29-34). New York: Continuum.

Shor, I. (1990). Liberation education: An interview with Ira Shor. *Language Arts, 67*(4), 342-353.

Shor, I. (1996). *When students have power: Negotiating authority in a critical pedagogy.* Chicago: University of Chicago Press.

Shor, I., & Freire, P. (1987). *A pedagogy for liberation: Dialogues on transforming education.* South Hadley, MA: Bergin & Garvey.

Shor, I., (Ed.). (1987). *Freire for the classroom: A sourcebook for liberatory teaching.* Portsmouth, NH: Boynton/Cook.

Shulman, J., & Mesa-Bains, A. (1993). *Diversity in the classroom: A casebook for teachers and teacher educators.* Hillsdale, NJ: Research for Better Schools & Lawrence Erlbaum Associates.

Silva, L. F. (2009). *O teatro do oprimido e Augusto Boal.* Retrieved May 31, 2009 from: http://www.pstu.org.br/cultura_materia.asp?id=10137&ida=0

Souto-Manning, M. (2005). *Critical narrative analysis of Brazilian women's schooling discourses: Negotiating agency and identity through participation in culture circles.* Unpublished doctoral dissertation. University of Georgia, Athens, GA.

Souto-Manning, M. (2007). Education for democracy: The text and context of Freirean culture circles in Brazil. In D. Stevick and B. Levinson (Eds.), *Reimagining civic* education: *How diverse nations and cultures form democratic citizens.* Lanham, MD: Rowman & Littlefield.

Souto-Manning, M. (2009a). Negotiating culturally responsive pedagogy through multicultural children's literature: Towards critical democratic literacy practices in a first grade classroom. *Journal of Early Childhood Literacy,* 9(1), 53-77.

Souto-Manning, M. (2009b). Critical narrative analysis of classroom discourse: Culture circles as a framework for empowerment and social action. In L. Jennings, P. Jewett, T. Laman, M. Souto-Manning, and J. Wilson (Eds.), *Sites of possibility: Critical dialogue across educational settings.* Cresskill, NJ: Hampton Press.

Souto-Manning, M. (2009c). Educating Latino children: International perspectives and values in early education. *Childhood Education,* 85(3), 182-186.

Souto-Manning, M., Cahnmann-Taylor, M., Dice, J., & Wooten, J. (2008). The power and possibilities of performative critical early childhood teacher education. *Journal of Early Childhood Teacher Education,* 29(4), 309-325.

Steiner, S., Krank, H., McLaren, P., & Bahruth, R. (2000). *Freirean pedagogy, praxis, and possibilities: Projects for the new millennium.* New York: Falmer Press.

Stubbs, M. (1996). Text and Corpus Analysis. In *Computer-assisted studies of language and culture.* Oxford, UK: Blackwell.

Sturge-Apple, M. L., Davies, P. T., & Cummings, E. M. (2006). Impact of hostility and withdrawal in interparental conflict on parental emotional unavailability and children's adjustment difficulties. *Child Development,* 77(6), 1623-1641.

Taylor, P. (1993). *The texts of Paulo Freire.* Buckingham: Open University Press.

Tegano, D., Groves, M., & Catron, C. (1999). Early childhood teachers' playfulness and ambiguity tolerance: Essential elements of encouraging creative potential of children. *Journal of Early Childhood Teacher Education,* 21, 291-300.

Tennant, M. (1995). *Learning and change in the adult years: A developmental perspective.* San Francisco: Jossey-Bass.

Tom, A. (1997). *Redesigning teacher education.* Albany: State University of New York Press.

Turner, R. H. (1960). Sponsored and contested mobility and the school system. *American Sociological Review,* 25(6), 855-867.

Valdés, G. (1996). *Con respeto: Bridging the distances between culturally diverse families and schools.* New York: Teachers College Press.

Vasquez, V. (2001). Constructing a critical curriculum with young children. In B. Comber and A. Simpson (Eds.), *Negotiating critical literacies in classrooms.* Mahwah, NJ: Lawrence Erlbaum.

Vasquez, V. M. (2004). *Negotiating critical literacies with young children.* Mahwah, NJ: LEA.

Villegas, A. M. (2007). Dispositions in teacher education: A look at social justice. *Journal of Teacher Education,* 58(5), 370-380.

Villenas, S., & Deyhle, D. (1999). Critical race theory and ethnographies challenging the stereotypes: Latino families, schooling, resilience, and resistance. *Curriculum Inquiry, 29*(4), 413-445.

Vygotsky, L. (1978). Mind in society: The development of higher psychological processes. Cambridge, MA: Harvard University Press.

Warnemuende, C. (1996). Stress/Burnout: Are you handling it effectively? *Montessori Life, 8,* 18.

Weis, L., & Fine, M. (2004). *Working method: Social justice and social research.* New York: Routledge.

Wertsch, J. V. (1991). *Voices of the mind: A sociocultural approach to mediated action.* Cambridge, MA: Harvard University Press.

Wiles, D. (2001). *Freedom summer.* New York: Atheneum.

Woodson, J. (2001). *The other side.* New York: Putnam's Sons.

Yamasaki, A., & Santos, E. (1999). A educação de jovens e adultos no Brasil: Histórico e desafios. In A. Yamasaki, E. Santos, L. do Nascimento, & S. Feitosa, *Cadernos de EJA 2: Educação de jovens e adultos, uma perspective freireana.* São Paulo, Brazil: IPF – Instituto Paulo Freire.

Index

About the Author

MARIANA SOUTO-MANNING, Ph.D., is Associate Professor of Early Childhood Education at Teachers College, Columbia University. From a critical perspective, she examines the sociocultural and historical foundations of schooling, language development, literacy practices, cultures, and discourses. She studies how children, families, and teachers from diverse backgrounds shape and are shaped by discursive practices, employing a methodology that combines discourse analysis with ethnographic investigation. Her work is published in journals such as *Early Child Development and Care, Early Childhood Education Journal, Journal of Early Childhood Research, Journal of Early Childhood Literacy, Journal of Research in Childhood Education*, and *Teachers College Record*. She was awarded the American Educational Research Association (AERA) Language and Social Processes Early Career Award in 2008 and the AERA Early Education and Child Development Early Research Career Award in 2009.

Photo: Andrew Davis Tucker